FAITH-NATURE-FAMILY

The Three-Threaded Cord of My Life

JEANETTE SEILING

ISBN: 978-0-9880993-4-0

Copyright © 2021 by Jeanette Seiling, updated April 2023.

All rights reserved.

No part of this book may be reproduced in any form or by any electronic or mechanical means, including information storage and retrieval systems, without written permission from the author.

*With gratefulness to my roots
And much love to my branches*

A three-threaded cord is not easily broken.

— ECCLESIASTES 4:12

CONTENTS

Foreword ix

1. My Life 1
2. Beginnings 3
3. Childhood 6
4. My Home 11
5. My Hometown 21
6. An Early Challenge 27
7. St. Jacobs Public School 30
8. Growing up in the 1960's 33
9. The Teen Years 36
10. Elmira District Secondary School 38
11. Off to University 41
12. Horsing Around 43
13. Have Wheels, Will Travel 50
14. I Met my Match 53
15. Lessons From My Parents 59
16. Practical Advice From my Mother 64
17. It's in the Genes 68
18. A Random Act of Kindness 74
19. Learning From my Grandparents 76
20. Ready For Children? 80
21. Letting Go 87
22. Parenting 90
23. Work 93
24. Pumpkin People 100
25. Travels beyond the "West" 103
26. A Trip with my Mother 107
27. Retirement 112
28. Call the Midwife 116
29. The COVID Pandemic 119
30. Photos are Great Memory Joggers 124
31. A Memorable Birthday 128

32. Golden Wedding Anniversary   130

RECOLLECTIONS

A Winner   135
Made to Shine, not Shrink   137
I Saw Naomi Dancing   141
Nature's Surround Sound   143
Creation   145
Advice for my Great Grandchildren (and Others)   147

Enough   149

FOREWORD

This book evolved from questions that popped into my email weekly from Storyworth, a program given to me by my children for my 70th birthday. The questions were random so when it came time to compile them into a book I tried to give some semblance of order to the different topics. That part took some effort. But what I became completely enthralled with, and at times absolutely lost in, were the memories of places, and people, and events that I had not thought of for years, maybe decades, which now rose from somewhere in the recesses of my mind and heart.

The writing of my childhood and my hometown, seeing once again in my mind the people and the nooks and crannies that were so dear to me, brought me much quiet pleasure.

I invite you into my memories of a simple but full life. I do hope you enjoy the stories. And perhaps, in later years when I can no longer remember, you could come and read these memories back to me. I think I would like that.

❦ 1 ❦
MY LIFE

I grew up amid the beautiful flowers of my mother's garden, and the rich earthiness of my father's fields of potatoes. Is it any wonder that through my life I have been drawn to the beauty and the importance of creation around me?

My earliest recollection of Sunday School is singing a song that I sang to my grandchildren many years later, as I rocked them to sleep:

> God sees the little sparrow fall
> It meets His tender view
> If God so loves the little birds
> I know he loves me too.

The song spoke to me when I was a child, reminding me of God's care for creation and His care for me. Later I learned *This is my Father's World,* a song of praise to God that is still sung at church gatherings, especially in the freshness of Springtime.

> This is my Father's world,
> And to my listening ears
> All nature sings, and round me rings
> The music of the spheres.
> This is my Father's world:
> I rest me in the thought
> Of rocks and trees, of skies and seas;
> His hand the wonders wrought.

Faith, nature, and family. Together in one bouquet.
That is how I was shaped and formed.
That is what has defined my life.

2
BEGINNINGS

Stories are the fabric of our lives, the threads that are woven together to make us who we are. This book tells the story of some of the threads of my life. Sometimes it is the little notes on scraps of paper that give hints to the story. Like the one inside a card sent to my mother after my birth. My aunt Naomi wrote "...hoping you feel a few degrees better than you did yesterday morning...and the baby is ok...just thinking if it was me I would have wanted (it) to come sooner too, just to know what's what."

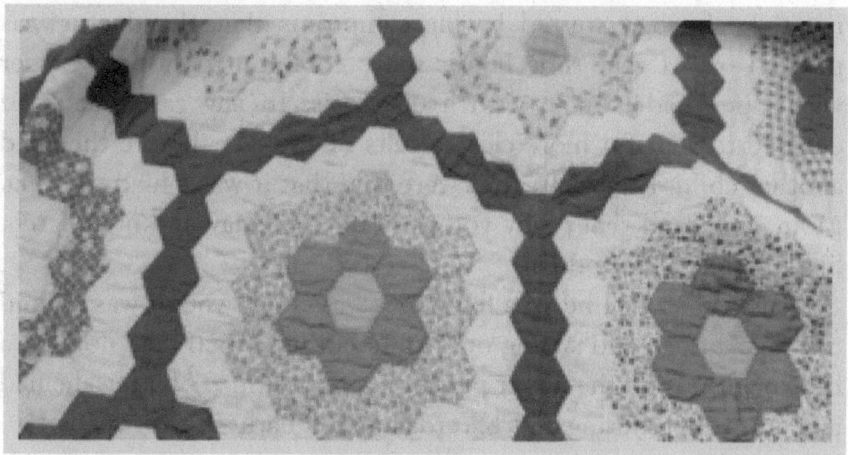

And the birth congratulations card that I chanced upon, from someone whose name I didn't recognize. On an otherwise sweet and flowery card she had written, "Sorry you did not get your boy but better luck next time." I was the third girl to be born to David and Elva, but really, who sends a baby card with a message like that?

I had heard, over the years, the story of my quick arrival. Mom told Naomi to run and get Daddy while she finished hanging out the laundry. The fast trip to the hospital. The nurse came, while Daddy was still signing the papers at admittance, to tell him that he had a new baby daughter.

Many decades later, in the weeks before Mom died, it seemed important to her that I should know why my birthday was in May, while both of my sisters had March birthdays. I really had not thought much about that. I just figured that happens. Not everyone in the family will have a birthday in the same month. But Mom told me that she had started having symptoms that the doctor was puzzled by. At that time it was more common to suspect cancer when they had trouble with a diagnosis. In any case, they had decided to wait for more clear results of the tests before they had another child. Eventually they were told that it was a hiatus hernia. Mom said, "and that's why you were born in May and not March, like Marlene and Linda."

Another story I heard a few times was about when I was around one year of age and sitting on Mom's lap in church. She noticed a brownish spot on the upper part of my right arm. Thinking she had just missed it during my Saturday night bath she proceeded to subtly give my arm a spit bath, rubbing the spot that would not go away. Over time that spot became bigger and browner and I remember being very self conscious about it. It is still with me, though faded somewhat, like the rest of me. It's a birthmark. And it really doesn't bother me at all anymore.

I have a few photos of myself as a baby and growing child. Just a few. I look quite cute with my dark brown, curly hair. I'm sure they weren't ashamed of me. It was just not common to take a lot of photos back in those days, and it was not common to tell children how cute and special they were. Somehow we knew we were special without the words. In my memory of those early years I picture a happy little girl with long braids and wearing my favourite "grasshopper" pants. A little girl so eager to meet this world that she pushed to arrive early, even before the laundry was all hung out. A little girl who was loved even though she was not a boy, but the third girl in the family.

Fishing with Daddy at the St Jacobs Dam circa 1954

3

CHILDHOOD

I was a child of the 1950's and I recall that in my early years I was often "working" alongside my parents and my sisters, especially in the summer when the gardens and the potato fields needed tending. But I also had lots of time to play. Compared to many children today, perhaps I had less toys, but I had a tricycle, and later a bicycle; a sleigh for wintertime fun; an outdoor little playhouse complete with furnishings, as much as 12 square feet could hold; a few cats and at times a puppy until Daddy said no more; and a doll or two that I usually played with only when my cousin Barbie wanted to play with it. Upstairs in the storeroom, squeezed in beside the hundred pound bag of sugar, there was a small desk where I could practice my letters or play teacher and expound on wise things to my attentive dolls.

There was a new entry room added on to our house when I was quite young, maybe five or six. In this addition there was a large window, and below it was a counter with two banks of drawers, one on each side of the piano stool seat. In the top drawer, on the right, was an odd collection of church bulletins, some keys, some other miscellany. Below that was a drawer for mittens and things. But the top drawer on the left was my drawer and in it I kept my special things. My treasures.

Photo of Abner and me. Mrs Schaner, my piano teacher, took this photo across the street from her house.

I have saved some of those special things. None of them have a high monetary value, or serve any real purpose anymore, but for some reason I have kept them for over sixty years. I guess I still enjoy the memories attached to them, because each piece has a story behind it.

There is a red plastic handkerchief box, a souvenir from a family trip to Virginia. While handkerchiefs were slowly being edged out in popular demand by the newcomer, Kleenex, they were still used by many, and were a common Christmas exchange gift. There is a turquoise flowered one that was from my friend Susannah and it reminds me of our walks together, down the railway tracks to school.

A little motion TV with a pencil sharpener in the back was the closest thing to a real television that we had at the time, and it only took a slight tipping back and forth and I could watch the man on the unicycle for hours, or as long as I wanted. A licence plate from my tricycle says Manitoba. I think I got it in a cereal box. The pink beaded brooch was a pretty thing that I never wore but liked to have.

A tiny Dennison box held star stickers. Stickers at that time were a rather rare commodity, used only in school for very good work or in Sunday School for attendance. Somehow I scrounged an empty box somewhere and in it I always kept my tiniest Bible, a Christmas gift from my Sunday School teacher, Mrs. Clayton Sauder, my aunt Naomi. The autograph book seems to be a relic from the past, but when I visited with an Old Order family recently I noticed that their young girls were writing in each other's books. Autograph books are a place to not only write your name, but also to impart words of wisdom. The messages in my book offered both the profound:

> As down the river of life you float
> May truth and honour guide your boat

and the mundane:

> I wish I wish I wish a-mighty
> I wish your pyjamas beside my nightie
> Now don't get excited, don't be misled
> I mean on the washline not in bed

Tiny dolls in their fabric cutout clothes are a reminder of my friend Sandra. Every recess time we would scuttle down the hill to the little copse of trees where, in the dirt, we had scratched the rooms for a house, and there we would design and craft new outfits for our dolls. These little bits of toys remind me of our friendship, and the simple joys of child's play.

CHILDHOOD

Marlene, Linda and I playing in the side lawn

One item notably missing from this collection is a folded up piece of paper that I always kept pretty far back in the drawer, under something else. I knew where it was, but it wasn't easily seen should someone for some reason open my top drawer. That paper held important information. On it I had sketched, as best I could, the genitalia of young kittens. This was important for when there was a new litter of kittens because I could simply refer to those sketches and then name the kittens appropriately. No more Toms becoming Thomasina or Henriettas needing to change to Henry.

"Top drawer." That was an expression we had, meaning it was the best. And the stuff of my young life, that I stored in my drawer, was all top drawer. I had more toys than just what fit into the top drawer. There was a monkey with a cap on. His name was DoJo. He's not around anymore.

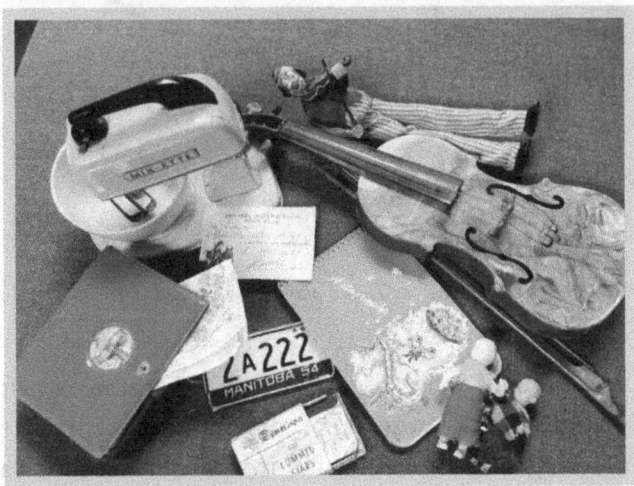

There was a clown on stilts who played a violin when he was wound up. I still have him for some reason. There was a toy mixmaster that I used in my playhouse until the batteries ran out. There was a top that spun wonderful patterns when I pressed down on the stem of it, and a marble roller that is still used by our grandchildren. And there was a pop gun rifle that somehow went missing over the years. It may have been found in the wreckage of the barn, so maybe it is at Kieswetter Demolition. Guns were something that I never allowed our children to have. Perhaps that was hypocritical but it seemed important for me, at the time when they were young, to take a strong stance for peace, and that meant no toy guns, even water pistols. In their teen years, when paintball was popular, I put the kibosh on that as well. I have a thing about guns, especially those that shoot deer. I'd rather put out salt licks for the deer and turn the guns into ploughshares or something. For the time in which I lived as a child, I was not at all deprived of toys or other amusements. Things were just different then than they are for children now.

4
MY HOME

The home where I grew up was quite different from the house into which my grandparents moved as a young couple. Over the years the house experienced the addition of an attached dwelling, and then several renovations to the interior. I liked the changes that my parents made. The memories of the special places in the house are ones that I hold dear.

There was a big porch at the front of the house. To the right was the door to Grandpa and Grandma Horst's house, and in the middle was our door. We didn't use that door very much, except to put the empty milk bottles on the bench, with a note and money for the next order of milk. Sometimes I would wait at the front window to see the milkman come with his faithful horse pulling the milk wagon. Sometimes other people came to the front door. Like a salesman. I think he sold Fuller Brush products,

but I'm not sure. He was a very assertive salesman who usually stuck his foot in the door as soon as it was opened. Mom didn't like this man and his insistent ways. It took me several years to know the reason why whenever we heard a knock at the front door Mom would grab my hand and we would hurry down to the cellar. And there we would stay until the knocking stopped and it was once again safe to go upstairs.

Most people came to our side door, the one shown in the photo. That main room was where the table and chairs were, and also the oil burner that helped to heat our house. That's where we had our weekly baths in a galvanized tub, filled with water which was drawn from the kitchen pump, and heated on the cookstove. I just vaguely recall those baths, and I wouldn't remember the pump except for a photo that I carried around in my wallet. It is a picture of my dad playing the accordion, and sitting in front of the kitchen sink and pump.

I don't remember the oil heater as well as I remember the register above it. After the oil heater left, it was through that register that I could listen in from upstairs to conversations when my parents thought I was sleeping.

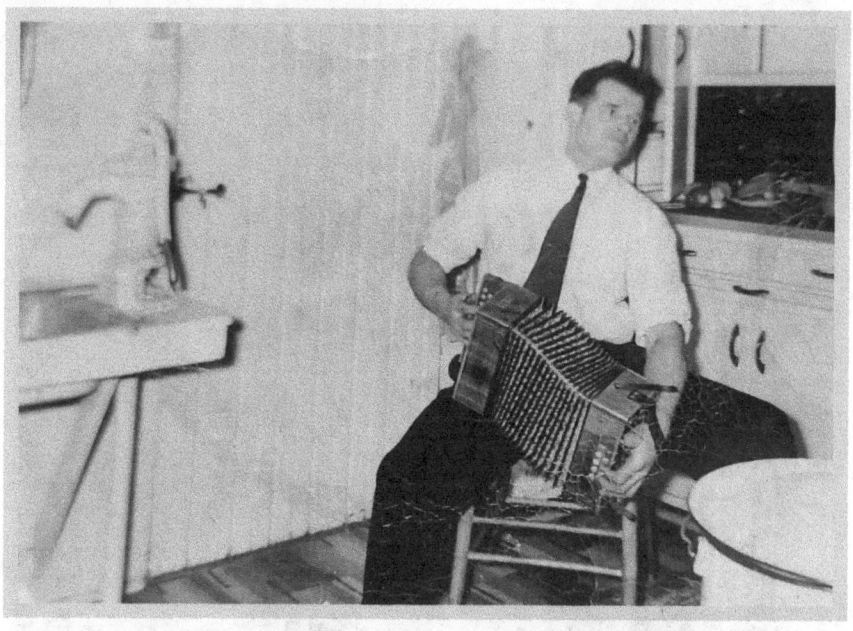

The kitchen was upgraded by closing off a door, leaving a window to see through, and that's when Mom got her new stove and fridge, I think. The stove had a broiler at the top where Daddy made his bacon every morning for breakfast. One egg, two slices of bacon, a piece of toast with jam, and a spoonful of applesauce to cut the grease. Something I found interesting in the cupboards was the flour bin and sifter. Mom did a lot of baking and that bin and sifter was a handy thing.

The main room was our dining room and that changed too when they built a small addition with a corner for my mother's sewing machine, a large window to look out on the world, a telephone nook with a bench seat, and the bank of drawers, one of which stored my special things.

Up one step from that main room was the living room. The biggest change there was the addition of a large bay window where Daddy would sit in the off-season to read his books and to watch the comings and goings.

There was also built-in shelving, and Mom picked out beautiful wool carpeting that I will always associate with home and the family gatherings that we had in that room. A piano was on the east wall, and next to the table of Mom's delicious food, the piano and accompanying instruments were central when family gathered.

My parents' bedroom was to the left of the living room. And then from there, with a quick rap on the door, I could go to visit my grandpa and grandma.

A stairway led up from the main room. At the top there was a window that looked out over the back yard. On the windowsill there was, at times, a large crown jar with elderberries, I was told, and lots of sugar in the bottom. For medicine, I was told. From this window I could watch the proceedings on chicken butchering day, if I wanted to. And usually after the first few chickens were placed, head between the two spikes on the wooden stump, followed by their decapitated bodies flopping drunkenly around the yard leaving a trail of blood as they went, I soon did not want to watch anymore.

The door straight ahead from the stairs landing opened to a storage room, which later became a bathroom. Next was my bedroom, which I think I first shared with Linda because I seem to remember two beds in there. My bedroom received an upgrade in my teen years adding a built-in desk and drawers, with shelves above, and a large closet. And then later, when my sisters were no longer at home, the wall was removed to make a large open room where Mom could display some of her paintings. Up one step, there was a very small store room (a place that it was interesting to snoop around in) and then at the end of the hall there were two bedrooms: one on the left that was Linda's and one on the right that was Marlene's. Sometimes I was invited into those rooms and sometimes I wasn't.

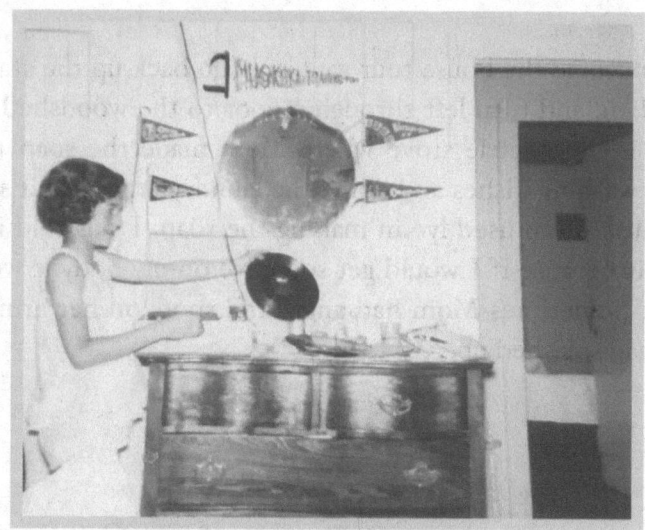

Back downstairs and through the kitchen to the left there was another stairway leading to the basement. There were lots of hooks along the stairway, a place for our outdoor work clothes, and our rubber boots went on a shelf to the right. And then in the basement - we called it a cellar - there was a wringer-washer that Mom used until they moved to St. Jacobs Place, the wash tubs, and the cistern. Daddy staunchly used rainwater whenever it was available. Only when the cistern was dry would we switch back to town water. Rainwater was soft water but sometimes had a musty odour of which I was not a fan. Water was treated as a fragile commodity, thus the calls up the stairsteps when we used more bathwater than was deemed necessary. I sometimes entertained dreams of what it might be like to luxuriate in a bathtub full of bubbly, scented water but that was not to happen under Daddy's watch. His water conservation was way ahead of the "Save The Water" programs that we have today.

Now back to the tour - against the cistern was the freezer, and across from that was an old cupboard where the canning jars were stored. Then through the doorway to a room for storage on the right and a room with shelves for canning on the left. In that room was also the stairway up to Grandpa and Grandma's side of the house.

To continue the house tour we would go back up the stairs, into the kitchen, and turn left through a door to the woodshed. To the left was a large kettle stove where Mom made the soap that she used for washing dishes and doing the laundry. It was a bit scary for me because Mom used lye in making the soap. I was told never to go near it because if I would get some lye on my body it would eat my skin. Sometimes Mom had angry red spots on her arms where the lye had splashed up.

There was a part of the woodshed that was deeper, down a couple steps, to a dirt floor. Wood was scattered there at random, having been pitched in through a small window the previous fall. But if you stayed on the upper part and turned to the right there was a door that led to a short sidewalk and just a few feet away was Grandma and Grandpa's house. This was my path when I wanted to play a game of Flinch or Lost Heir or maybe just talk with their Budgie bird, Peter. (In my teen years there was yet another renovation to this room that closed off this door. My Grandma cried about that. Maybe she felt closed off. But the woodshed became a pine-walled, braided mat haven. With a Franklin woodburning stove and all of Mom's decorating touches, it became a cozy place for grandchildren sleepovers, or just to gather.)

Turning left instead of going out that door, another small door led to a tiny, little room in the corner, and that was our "outdoor plumbing" or "outhouse". I forget if it was a one-seater or if it had two seats. People talk about having to use newspaper for cleanup in those days, but I seem to remember a roll of toilet paper on a curved piece of steel, nailed to the wall. There was a calendar on the wall, in case we needed to know what the date was as we spent time there. Just decoration I suppose.

Cousins eating together in the Woodshed circa 1982. After the renovation we still referred to the room as "The Woodshed"

A NEW BATHROOM!

I think one of the biggest changes to the house was getting a modern bathroom. In my very early years bathroom conveniences were very basic. We had a small sink in the kitchen where we pumped water to wash up or, if we were coming in from working in the garden, we washed at the big pump outside. Baths were taken in a large tub of water set beside the oil heater in the main downstairs room.

Then, when I was about five years old, some carpenters came to rip apart our upstairs storeroom - that room with the shelves full of stuff and the 100 pound bag of sugar pushed up against my school desk where I did my important work - and they were going to make it into a new bathroom for us. A sink with running water! A bathtub with much more room than the galvanized tub downstairs beside the oil heater, and the tub was good even if Daddy said, "No more than two inches of water in there!" And then there was the toilet with a flusher. A big change. This was high living! By all signs, we had arrived. That is the house as I remember it, but the outbuildings were also important to me.

OUTBUILDINGS

The main barn was a large structure painted a "barn red" colour, touched up every few years with Daddy's instructions for painting: "Not too peticulah. Chust slap it on." The front part of the barn was used as a garage for the car, a tool shed, a tractor shed, and a little outhouse at the end. (That outhouse now lives on our property, not used for its original purpose but more as a decorative feature.) The back of the barn was for chickens, or my science project sheep, or my horse and pony, and also some steers one year to help keep the horses warm. The upstairs of the barn had been for chickens in earlier years but was later used as storage for scrap lumber that Daddy hauled from Fairway Lumber, some of it just too beautiful to burn. In my early years I had used one of the rooms for playing school and found the chicken coops useful for keeping school work and books.

Daddy built an addition onto the barn for potato storage, bushel basket storage, and a place where we cut potatoes for spring planting. There was also a root cellar where potatoes were stored for winter sales. That was one of the places where I helped to sort the good from the bad, aided only by the light of a kerosene lamp, and sometimes got the surprise of a finger poked into a rotten potato. I can smell it as I write.

To the right of the barn were smaller buildings that started out as chick and chicken barns. I remember the times that the baby chicks came and we watched them on their clean wood shavings, huddled under the brooder lamps and sometimes waddling over to the feeders or waterers. They were so cute. They were less cute when they were grown and when, after dark, we needed to catch them by their legs and carry them to the big barn for roomier accommodation.

I remember Daddy having a flashlight in his mouth and grabbing about four chickens in each hand and heading to the barn, gagging on the flashlight. Some things I would rather forget.

My dad and five other potato growers built a potato storage barn at the back of the property. I was about 10 at the time and remember having good times with my cousin who was from Virginia but up for the summer to help. He amused me by "balking tackwards" and we made up stories about the men building the storage. And then, on a hot summer's day, when the work was done, we would head back to Lion's Hole for a swim. But that's another story.

Trigger, Alfred, Shippy, Ramsey and me. Summer 1964

❦ 5 ❦
MY HOMETOWN

I have moved just once in my life, from the Doddy house of my parent's home, to the farmhouse where I have lived now for forty-seven years. I am a homebody. I don't move around a lot.

Painting by Mom 1976, which I commissioned with inheritance money from my grandparents

The village of St. Jacobs is where I grew up. Technically it's a village, but we always referred to it as a town. In my early years, St. Jacobs was a quiet little village where most everyone knew each other, and looked out for one another. A place where a child could walk freely to school, or to the library, or to the baseball park at the other end of the village. The population was growing and by 1959 there were about 725 people. But it was still small enough that we knew almost everyone, some better than others.

We lived at the south end of St. Jacobs, just two houses before Johnny Snyder's Texaco Service Station, going out of town. Ours was a big house, consisting of the main larger dwelling plus a Doddy house. It was one of the older homes in town. My grandparents had moved into it in the early years of their marriage.

Between our house and the Texaco Service Station was a brown brick house that my uncle Noah had built. Daddy said he was a notcher, a very particular carpenter, so probably everything about that house was well constructed. Later, before I was born, Uncle Noah built another house down the back street to the school so my cousin Barbie and I never lived right beside each other.

On the other side of us was an older couple, the Cress', Harold and Olga. Harold at one time worked in Smitty's Shoe factory with my dad. They were nice people. Mrs. Cress made tiny little felt pairs of mittens that had a hair clip in them to use as a bookmark and she gave one of them to me. I might still have it.

Dolly Martin was a daughter of Johnny Snyder and she lived across the street in a new house. She worked at Home Hardware a lot of her life. She knew much of what went on in the village of St. Jacobs and later she gathered all of that information into an interesting book. Dolly's husband, Oscar, walked a lot. He was a quiet man who smoked a pipe and squinted with one eye, especially when he smiled. Everyday, at the exact same time, he set out with his hiking pole and was often gone for quite some time. I imagine that he would have been able to add quite a bit to Dolly's book about all that he observed on his walks.

Next to them, and directly across the road from our house, were the Webers. In my child's mind they were study-worthy because they seemed different, at least different from us. From my sister's upstairs bedroom window I had a good vantage point and could look down from there to view their comings and goings.

Mr. Weber had an office job as a bookkeeper, I was told, and every day at the same time he would back his car out of the garage and head south in the direction of Waterloo. Every day between 5:30 and 6 o'clock he would arrive back home, and drive into his garage. I didn't usually see him outside unless he was mowing the lawn on Saturday. He was a man of routine.

On Sunday, the whole family would get into the car and head down the road towards Waterloo, most likely to church. But I wondered, with three churches in our village - Mennonite, Lutheran, and Evangelical United Brethren - where did they go to church? I didn't know.

But the best part was the children. They were a lot older than I. There was a boy and three girls. I don't remember much about the boy, but I do remember the girls. Their names were Jean, Joan, and Julianne. Jean and Joan were twins. At one time my paper dolls were named after these fascinating neighbours. I loved to watch on a Friday evening as their boyfriends would come and, one by one, the beautiful girls, in their beautiful dresses, would drive away with their very handsome dates.

I didn't need TV because every Friday night, from the second-storey bedroom window that faced their house, I could watch them and let my imagination fill in the story of their lives. They lived just across the road from me, but it sometimes seemed that we were worlds apart.

The next house was where Sally's family lived. She was in my grade at school, but we didn't often play together. She and Brenda, two houses down, walked to school together. I didn't often join them because I went the back way, and besides, three's a crowd.

Late one night I heard a car stop and there was loud talking. I went to the window to investigate. Sally's father had gotten out of a car and was shouting to the other people in the car and then he made his way across the road and down the driveway to his house. He was wobbly when he walked. My dad didn't ever wobble when he walked. Sally's house had only one floor, no stairs to climb up to her bedroom.

One time Brenda's dad asked me and some other girls to serve at a Lion's Club dinner at the Dominion Hotel downtown. I had never before been in a hotel, and I wasn't sure what a Lion's Club was. It was later in my teen years when I was working the Friday night shift at the Mill End store, across the street from the hotel, that I again had the opportunity to observe the comings and goings and had further insight into a different way of life than my father chose to live.

Our church was about a block and a half from our house. Church services, Sunday School classes, Daily Vacation Bible School, and later youth groups were not far away. A good thing because much of my growing up years involved the church and church friends.

The post office was in the middle of the village. Our address was Box 113 and we had a key for that little cubbyhole of a mailbox. Marvin Smith was our friendly postman, and it was from him that I sought guidance in my postage stamp collection stage. Daddy drove down for the mail most days, but sometimes I would run down to get it. In hindsight I wonder what the neighbours thought of this girl who ran down the sidewalk blocks. Always running. I suppose that habit stood me in good stead when I started competing in track events. Running was just what I did, and I wish I still could run.

The harness shop was across the street from the post office. Mr. Voelzing once made a halter for Shippy, the mottle-faced lamb that I was trying to train to walk by leash, as part of my grade seven science project.

Down one block, at the next corner, was the blacksmith shop. It was there that I would ride my horse and then Jonathan Martin trimmed Roco's hoofs and re-nailed the shoes. When Roco had started to limp, Mr. Martin tried to help the problem by packing his hooves with a tar-like substance.

We had two grocery stores in town. Quite convenient for all the villagers and also for the Old Order Mennonite farmers in the surrounding countryside.

The library was on the same backstreet as the school. I went there quite a bit, but now can only remember one book that I signed out as a child, *Little Black Sambo*. That is a book that probably would not be allowed in a library anymore.

The train station was back one more street. That's where Daddy and I went in the springtime to pick up the seed potatoes that were shipped by train from Prince Edward Island. Daddy propped our toboggan up against a wall while he loaded the bags of potatoes. We then forgot about the toboggan and it was no longer there when he returned.

Up the hill at the north end of the village was the ball diamond and park, often used for our annual church picnic. Different leagues used the ball diamond, including the Mennonite Church league. It was a good source of entertainment in my teen years.

It was a homey little village. A mostly homogeneous one as well. But not everyone was exactly like my family, I noticed. There was a boy at school who lived in an upstairs apartment with just a mother.

I wondered about that. One year there was one Indigenous (we called them Indian) boy, and I happened to hear that he was living with a family in town for the year, but his real home was in Northern Ontario. There were also Old Order Mennonite and Markham Mennonite children in my school. Parochial schools were not started until 1964/65.

When I was a bit older I heard my dad talking about the Second World War when some people in town hated the Mennonite boys for not going to war. I didn't feel hatred from my Lutheran and Evangelical friends.

For the most part we lived happily together, the three churches working together each summer for two weeks of Daily Vacation Bible School, and taking turns hosting the Easter Sunrise Service. If there were differences that I perceived, my shyness prevented me from asking too many questions, even of my parents.

These are the places that were important to me when I was growing up in St. Jacobs. As I write this description of the village in the years of my childhood, I can't help but think of all the changes that have happened since then. Not least of all, the home that held so many memories is no longer there. That lot now is the home of Tim Horton's. I don't often drive past there.

6
AN EARLY CHALLENGE

When I think back on my childhood I remember the carefree and pleasant life of a loved and cared for young girl. There is one experience, however, that sticks out as a particularly scary and unpleasant time. It was Easter Weekend 1958, decades ago, but some memories stick for a long time.

I was born with a birthmark on the back of my head. My hair covered it up, but when I was about 7 the birthmark started to grow. They say that the sense of hearing is strong, but I know that the sense of touch is also strong because as I write about this I get the same squiggly feeling in my stomach that I got every time I reached back and slipped my finger under the bottom of that birthmark. The doctor said it had to be removed and my surgery was scheduled for Easter weekend. I was an adult when Mom talked to me about their fear that it was a cancerous tumour. I had never been to a hospital, so I imagine that I didn't worry too much because I didn't know what to worry about. That changed.

I was a very shy girl and there were several times that Mom missed out on things because she needed to stay with me. But staying with me in the hospital was not an option. This was a generation before parents were allowed to stay with their children in the hospital. So I was put into a children's ward with several other young children. And my parents left.

In that hospital ward I was desperately lonely and scared. I was too scared to get up to use the bathroom, and the result was wet bottoms of the babydoll pajamas that Mom had made for me. The nurse changed the sheets and washed out the bottoms and hung them on the lower rung of the bed. That made sense to her, I guess, but she didn't know that one of the boys saw the bottoms and taunted me for wetting. I'm sure I cried, although I don't remember.

I have a clear memory, however, of going into the operating room and having the anesthesiologist explain to me that he was going to put me to sleep. He told me that I should count backwards with him, from one hundred down to one, and then I would be asleep. I did not want to go to sleep, so I held my breath. I'm pretty sure I hastened the effect of the anaesthetic.

AN EARLY CHALLENGE

The post-op is something that is no longer clear in my memory, but it probably involved throwing up from that anaesthetic that I failed to avoid. Mom had always been with me for times like that, but not then.

Somehow I survived and I was so relieved to be going home on Easter Sunday morning. Except that Mom and Daddy did not come to get me in the morning like the other parents came for their children. Apparently my parents went to church instead. Something that I later understood, but something that did not at all make sense at the time.

The whole experience was traumatizing for my not quite 8-year-old self. I went home with a cone-shaped bandage on the back of my head, that was not too easy to sleep with but it protected the site of the surgery. With little effort, I can still feel my tight face as the skin stretched back to close the surgical site. I have a box with my braids that had to be cut off, and a scar on the back of my head that necessitates rearranging my hair in the wind or for the people sitting behind me in church.

But there was something that I carried home from the hospital. A big Chocolate Easter Bunny from Uncle Mel and Aunt Leeta. Bigger than any I had ever had. That was the light at the end of my dark tunnel.

I think of this experience most Easter seasons. Alongside the experience of the suffering Christ it is minimal, but in the life of this young girl it was huge. This year I sent a thank you letter to Leeta just in case I hadn't thanked them before.

P.S. After I sent that very belated thank you to Aunt Leeta she called and told me that she had a feeling that I had already thanked them. She is an avid diary keeper so she turned to those records, and there, in 1996, she had written that when they came home from a brief time away they found a chocolate Easter bunny, complete with a thank you note, tucked between their doors.

※ 7 ※
ST. JACOBS PUBLIC SCHOOL

I started school in 1956. At that time there was no kindergarten class in our school. Maybe just in the cities.

Grades 3-4, taken in front of the school. I am in the front row, third from the right. I am surprised that I can remember the names of all but two of my classmates.

The school was about three and one half blocks from our house, so it was an easy walk. My sister, Linda, would have still been at the same school so I imagine that she walked with me those first days. I enjoyed walking to school, sometimes down the main street. Those were the days when I went home for lunch, and then on my return to school I sometimes stopped at Amos Bowman's store for one of their huge ice cream cones.

Other times, I walked down the back street. Going that way was good, except for passing this one house where there was an old man who scared me. His house was run down, and he dressed in shabby clothes, and didn't smile. Some days I crossed the street when I got near his house and then, like a shot out of a cannon, I ran until I was on the school property. My friend Sandra was also a bit scared of him and when we were older and braver we conspired to be friendly to Leander. We started with little steps and gradually we took courage to go close to his house porch, and then one day we talked with him. After that I didn't run past his house, but instead I slowed down and, if I could see him anywhere, I smiled and waved to him.

Little did I know that one day my mother would attend his auction sale and buy the baby cradle that each of our children and grandchildren have slept in.

My grade one teacher was Mrs. Hunsberger, the wife of the photographer in town, as I later found out. Our grade one classroom was part of a new addition that had just been added onto the original school building. There were four classrooms in that new wing, and the grade one class was at the end of the hall. I remember doing work in our  *Think and Do* or *Do and Learn* books, and learning to read in the Dick and Jane series of books.

I liked most of my teachers and noted different characteristics of each of them. I was concerned about one teacher for a while because after she blew her nose the Kleenex would be a bit red. I thought there was something terribly wrong, but it turned out that it was her bright red lipstick that wiped off a bit. Lipstick! I didn't know much about that. There was so much more to learn than just schoolwork. She was the same teacher who made me stand in the corner out in the hall because I pulled Sandra's braid back to try to put it into the inkwell in my desk. I had to stand there while the grade eight class and the principal just happened to troop by. So embarrassing! And there wasn't even ink in the well.

Another teacher kept us all enthralled guessing what colour her hair would be when she came to school on Monday. Purple, blue, pink, green? This was before hair colouring became popular. Apparently she had some kind of rinse that she put on her hair on the weekend, and sometimes it worked better than other times.

My grade eight teacher had pronounced that Friday would be a day of reading comprehension tests and reciting memory work and for piano students to take turns playing *God Save The Queen* during morning exercises. I did not always comprehend stories so well and I did not like reciting poetry in front of the class and I especially didn't like playing the piano in front of the class. I did not like Fridays.

But there were better things ahead. At least I hoped so.

8
GROWING UP IN THE 1960'S

Turning ten years old in 1960 was the first time that I felt that I had "arrived" (the next time wouldn't happen until I was turning seventy). And I don't know what that feeling was about, except that turning ten seemed to hold such possibility, such hope of great things to come.

In our family there was never a lot of fanfare over birthdays. I remember one party when I was young, and I remember one year there were coins hidden within the chocolate layer cake. Maybe that was the year I turned ten.

I imagine that I had outgrown my grasshopper pants by then, but just barely. I hung on to those lined-with-plaid-flannel, javex-smelling denims until long after their best before date. (I know. You can't see my grasshopper pants in the photo above but I know that I was wearing them when Daddy took this picture.)

Dolls had been put on the back burner and I was getting deeper into my tomboy stage. That stage lasted for most of the 60s, but not quite all.

I started to broaden my interests in the world around me, and I remember feeling a fair bit of angst. Not just how-do-I-get-out-of-taking-piano-lessons angst, but fear of what I was hearing about the Cold War; what was going to happen if Russia bombed us; how could President Kennedy be shot; and what would happen if I never got my period because my cousin told me I could never have children then. That kind of angst.

I confided all of this to my pony, Trigger, but aside from nodding his head at the appropriate or, more likely, inappropriate times, he had little to offer in the way of wisdom or even a basic show of support.

The Beatles and Elvis Presley were very popular; there was growing unrest in the Deep South between the white supremacists and the blacks; troubles were brewing within Canada as Quebec threatened to separate and split up our country. I wrote a rather passionate essay about that for my grade 12 history class to which the teacher commented that "it was well worth all the trouble you've been the rest of the year." I regret that I was too timid to ask him about that comment.

Canada turned 100 in 1967 and we travelled to Mel and Leeta's and then sashayed from there into Montreal for Expo '67. It was slated as an incredible celebration of Canada and the world. Cousin Doug and I were let loose on our own, and our top mission was to go to as many country tents as we could to get as many stamps in our passports as we could. The displays by each of the countries were probably wonderful. I will never know.

9
THE TEEN YEARS

The teen years are known to be that time when youth are trying to "find themselves" - who am I? where do I fit in? It's a time when they are prone to following certain trends or fads, as they may be called.

A fad is defined as "an intense, widely spread enthusiasm for something." For example, the hula hoop and poodle skirts of the 50s, the gogo boots and hippie logos of the 60s (including peace signs on VW vans), Rubik's cubes, bell bottoms, mini skirts and pet rocks of the 70s. Many of these fads were short lived, some popped up again years later, and a few became a part of some people's lives forever.

Growing up I tended to be a more conservative type, and didn't latch onto a lot of fads. There were, of course, a few exceptions.

Mom was a seamstress extraordinaire, with the ability to reproduce any fashion currently in vogue. In my early years that included modest changes to the neckline, or the drape of a dress or some other means of making "homemade clothing" avant garde. One creation that I remember was the poodle skirt that she made for me when I was maybe eight. I still have a scrap of the mottled blue felt, and somewhere there is a brown felt dog with carefully embroidered features that she had handsewn just above the hem on the left side. Poodle skirts were very popular at that time, if not even a fad. I loved that skirt.

In my teen years I began to do my own sewing and was able to replicate the bell bottom pants, and later the palazzo pants that were the craze. These styles are presently experiencing another resurgence.

Hula hooping was a thing. Something I amused myself with at home, and at school with classmates. Apparently my body saw it as a short term fling and today refuses to acknowledge that it ever knew how to move to the hula rhythm.

10

ELMIRA DISTRICT SECONDARY SCHOOL

My High School sweater. I earned the Senior Letter, mostly in sports.

I n the fall of 1964, I caught the school bus just past my house, and started grade nine at Elmira District Secondary School. Some of my friends from church went to Rockway Mennonite High School in Kitchener. My sisters had gone there too, but when my parents gave the choice, I chose EDSS.

We were very "streamed" in those years, needing to make course choices in grade eight that would set the path for our five years of secondary school, and ultimately our future career ambitions. I think we had some guidance for choosing, but it was minimal. I chose 5-year Arts and Science, and made other decisions for electives within that framework. That stream had no provision for typing class or other business courses. Perhaps if I had one of those typing courses I could use a computer keyboard just a little bit better, maybe good enough to keep up with my younger grandchildren now.

Captain of the senior girls' basketball team

I enjoyed Secondary School and excelled until grade 11 when the work got harder, but I didn't study harder. In ninth grade we were all expected to go out for track and field day. I raced and jumped and threw, and my gym teacher noticed that athletics came easily for me. Probably all those years of running everywhere. In my first track and field meet I racked up enough wins to become the Girls' Junior Track and Field champion, and then kept up the competition for the following four years, adding two more years of female champion to my name. I felt sick before each meet, but I kept it up. Daddy wondered why I did it and gave me no encouragement to continue. Perhaps there is more competitive spirit in me than I like to admit.

By the end of my last year of secondary school my marks were good enough to get me into the University of Waterloo, and I was following my desire to study to be a probation officer.

11
OFF TO UNIVERSITY

As the 1960s drew to a close, I was off to the new adventure of university, and the world, at least my part of it, was looking good.

University was a whole different world from elementary and secondary school. The main campus seemed huge in itself and then there were church colleges across the creek as well. I had enrolled in entry level courses, six of them that first fall. Some classes were very large, held in an amphitheatre, and others were small and intimate. I preferred to get lost in the large classes, but learned that environment was not the best place to get individual help.

My English class was small and our only assignment was a portfolio of our writings at the end of the term. I worked hard at it, including some previous work from high school, but mostly new writings. The professor had told us to come to his office after term to pick up our portfolio if we wanted it back. I was hesitant to do that because I lacked confidence that any of my "stuff" was good. Later, when I got my term marks back I saw that I had gotten an A+. Today I would love to have that portfolio. It would be a capsule of my thinking and writing at that period in my life.

Another class in which I enrolled was Anthropology. I can

remember at the time being concerned that the course content was not in line with the teachings that I had in the church. My mark reflected that hesitancy to learn more about it. Now, in my mature years, I think that same course would be fascinating.

In the first two years I concentrated on sociology and psychology courses. Of all my university courses, the one where I had a failing grade was Juvenile Delinquency. I had trouble understanding the professor and his expectations, and it was a very large class. I was upset with myself for messing up the one and only test there was for the term.

I was disappointed partly because of my bad mark, but mostly because of the topic that I had felt was necessary for my future career. How could I pursue my dream of being a probation officer if I couldn't even pass an exam in Juvenile Delinquency? Little did I know that in a few short months my direction in life would change. Marriage, children, and then back to school as a mature student to finish my BA, finally graduating in 1991.

❧ 12 ❧
HORSING AROUND

Roped in and around my schooling was life with my horses. Introversion was not in my vocabulary in my early years, but the signs were probably there. I didn't beg for friends to come over. Few playdates for me. In fact, we didn't know what playdates were back then. But I developed a love for horses, and I can't remember exactly but I think it was those early days with Dan Kraemer's young colts that started the romance.

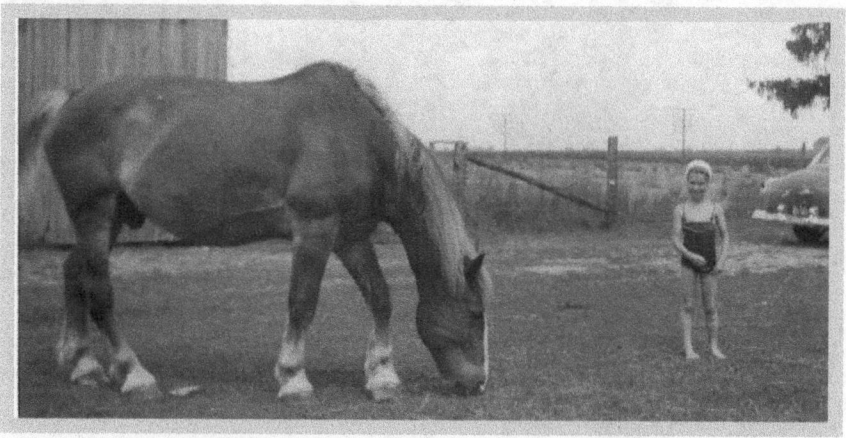

I had used the fallow lot near the potato storage building to practise sports - setting up a makeshift high jump for track and field events or pitching a baseball against the building to hone my skills during baseball season. It was a place where I could be alone, doing what I wanted to do.

And then one day Dan put up a snow fence paddock, and the next day he led out two young foals. I watched them cavort around, shyly coming toward me, and then quickly galloping off again. I was smitten.

I thought about them when I should have been doing homework. I doodled horse heads in my notebooks. I dreamed about what it would be like to have my own horse one day.

Dan Kraemer owned Kraemer Woodworking, a business that backed onto our family's property. Dan was an older gentleman, a cousin of my dad's, but unlike Daddy his family had remained with the Old Order Mennonite community so he drove a horse and buggy. Dan and his wife lived in the house across Henry Street from the woodworking establishment, and the barn where he kept his horse was beside the wood shop. Dan used a horse for transportation and the young colts stayed in the barn with his driving horse and then during the day they frisked around in the paddock behind the shop. And this is where I, as a young girl, started my love affair with horses.

A visit to those foals required only a run through our backyard, a jump over the strawberry patch, a skip past a row of beans, and then a careful trot through the pumpkin patch (careful because I should not step on the vines because that would hinder the growth of more pumpkins) and then I was at the fence and able to watch those young, equine beauties frisking and frolicing about, kicking up their heels with joy.

At first it took a bit of time for them to be brave enough to approach me. I would call them, offer a handful of grass, and do anything to encourage them, but they had to get to know me, to trust me. Before long Dan saw me with the horses, and noticed that I had a keen interest. Sometimes, when his workday was over, he would come into the paddock and lead one of the foals over to me so that I could pet it. He told me about the horses, taught me how to brush them, and later allowed me to lead them around in the pen. I got to know the horses, and Dan too. We became friends, and when I would take the shortcut to school, by going through our garden and then through the woodworking property, I'd often spot Dan in his office, and we'd wave to each other.

In the summer just after my twelfth birthday, I went to Central Ontario Pony Club at the riding stables near the Pioneer Tower, at the south end of Kitchener. (Many years later, when Ron took me to my first Seiling Christmas at his Aunt Val's, I recognised the stables. They lived in the house on the same property).

I don't remember much about the pony club experience. Maybe I went with my friend Connie because I know she had a pony and I don't think I would have gone by myself, without knowing anyone. I do remember that we learned the parts of a horse, and for homework we needed to draw a horse and label the parts. Then the instructor taught us how to clean the tack. We learned to ride English style, with an English saddle, and the English style of turning the horse's head by pulling on the reins in the direction that we wanted to go. And posting. I loved posting. When the horse is trotting, the rider bounces a lot and it can be rather uncomfortable, both for the rider and the horse. Posting is an up-and-down motion in rhythm with the horse's strides. And it's like riding a bicycle. Once you learn it, you don't forget it. Anytime when I have the opportunity now to ride a horse, the posting is automatic and much more comfortable for my aging body.

Later, when I got my Western horse (with a brand on his rump to prove it), I bought a Western saddle and neck-reined, having both reins in one hand and laying them over the horse's neck to turn. Western saddles seem more secure because they have a pommel at the front that is handy to hold on to when you are at a full gallop and need extra control.

When I was twelve my wish for a horse of my own came true. Daddy had heard of a horse for sale at the north end of town. We drove there on a summer evening to see it. For some reason Daddy drove the car into the pasture where the horse was. That car was pretty special. A white station wagon, with wood grain panels along the sides. He was pretty proud of it. But the problem was that the horse was moonblind, meaning it could see only shadows. When we were examining the horse it walked close to the car and brushed the tender part, just in front of its hind leg, on the back corner of the car. The horse lashed out with both back feet and left an imprint of two hooves on the back end of Daddy's car. I thought it was game over for ever buying that horse and was very surprised that my father went ahead with the purchase. A horseman that Daddy knew rode the horse from the north end of town to our barn at the south end of town. He said the horse handled beautifully. Daddy and I made another trip, this time to Keleher's Saddlery near Cambridge, and I picked out a black Western saddle with lots of nickel studs, and a bridle and martingale to match. Maybe that is where I got my riding boots too. I tallied this all up in my notebook where I kept track of expenses.

Getting almost too big for Trigger

My dad loved horses but confessed that he was afraid of them, and that didn't bode well for a horse that was particularly sensitive to touch and nervousness of people. It was trained to go faster when the rider squeezed her legs. I got along fine with it, but when my sister rode she hung on tightly with her legs and then pulled back on the reins when the horse started running. The horse was confused, and Daddy no longer felt safe. When the horse reared up into a cherry tree with Linda holding on for dear life, Daddy said this was not the horse for us. I wish I could remember the name of that horse.

I think it was with Dan's help that we got a lead on a twelve-hand pony, the perfect size for me, at least for a while. He was part Welsh, part Shetland, and part Hackney, which meant that he lifted his knees up when he trotted. Maybe he had been a show pony because, with a little encouragement, he would stand with his front and back legs stretched out, and his head held high. He looked sharp. I spent a lot of time grooming, riding, and mucking out, and if truth be told, Daddy probably did more mucking out than I did.

Trigger was trained to be ridden, or to pull a carriage or sleigh. I rode him a lot, until I was too tall. The sleigh rides were good winter fun, and I remember one ride with the two-seater cart when I took Mom and her friend Agnes, along with their paint boxes and easels, to do some plein air painting in the countryside just past the St. Jacobs dam. Trigger stayed for a while after I bought Roco, and then we sold him to an Amish family to drive their children to school.

Roco was a beautiful jet-black, 15 ½ hand gelding. We spent a lot of time travelling the countryside together. South, then east on the "dump road", then down the hill to Abner Good's flats, and then home on the back street of St. Jacobs. Another evening we would head west on the road back to the dam, and sometimes from there we'd head to the Three Bridges road, and into Hawkesville. That little burg was a quiet, sleepy place in those years. The hoofbeats echoed as we clip-clopped our way, curtains were brushed aside to view who was coming through town, and on we'd go, coming back past our church cemetery, turning east into St. Jacobs, and then home.

Roco, my 15 1/2 hand black gelding

I loved the solitude of those rides. My horses became my close friends in the years when I needed "someone" to listen.

❧ 13 ❧
HAVE WHEELS, WILL TRAVEL

While my preferred mode of transportation was riding a horse, that was not possible for everything. In the summer of '69, when I was anticipating heading off to university, I got my first car. I remember the year because my university number is indelibly imprinted on the part of my brain that is supposed to remember things like that - 69040424. That number jumps to the head of the line almost every time I need to remember a bank account number, an address, or a password. Like a child in line for a popsicle, there it is, front and centre.

So, my brother-in-law had a friend who had a car. His friend wanted to sell that car. It was dark blue and small, just big enough for taxiing two of my friends and me to and from university. I took it on a test run, I think, because you always do that before you purchase a vehicle, and I bought it.

That first major investment of mine was a rare type. A foreign car, quite probably a British Ford product. Perhaps an Anglia. Apparently the repair parts for such a car were not widely available, but I was not planning to need repair parts for it.

For the most part the car worked fine, as far as I was concerned.

It got us where we wanted to go, and my friends chipped in for the gas money. A win-win situation, one would think.

But all was not as well as I thought. Apparently I was not operating the clutch properly, and apparently my brother-in-law heard, on different occasions, that I was doing some grinding of gears, or riding of the clutch, or a combination of both, which would be worse. This was not good, and could ultimately result in the need for some of those special repair parts, not widely available.

It got us through our first year, but then I sold it to someone who then drove it for years. Apparently she knew how to properly operate the clutch. No special parts required.

During the summers between university years, I worked for Family and Children's Services in Guelph and made trips to Sick Kids in Toronto, to Windsor for appointments, to camps in northern Ontario. I needed a different vehicle. One that was larger, newer, reliable, and had no clutch!

Daddy and I went to Mitchell Motors in Elmira to check out a new vehicle that they were advertising. It was American Motors' "corporate genius". A subcompact car touted to cost only two-thirds the price of a regular car. A great selling point. The critics said that the price made sense because it was only two-thirds of a car. Yes, it looked like a car with its back end chopped off, but I liked it. I lean towards things that are a little different, and this car fit the bill.

We talked with the handsome salesman. I remember liking the cologne he was wearing. Daddy was not one to shop around and weigh a number of different options so we bought it then and there.

It was a Gremlin. White, with red rally stripes down the sides. I brought it home and parked it behind the barn, where it stayed for awhile. Was I embarrassed? Not at all. I do the same thing when I buy a sweater, or a new dress, or whatever. I bring it home, and I lay it out on the couch, or the bed, and I admire it for a bit. Perhaps I audition a pair of pants or a scarf with it. Perhaps I just let it lie there till we get used to each other. Later that week, or maybe the next week, I will wear it. So it was with the car. Eventually, maybe the next day, I brought it out for a drive.

Many scoffed at my "part of a car". Its main selling feature was that it was a small car, but it handled like a big car. I thought its main feature was its looks. It may have looked a bit cut off at the back, or perhaps that some big truck had smashed into its rear, but I loved it. Not many agreed. Least of all my future husband. I met Ron that first summer of the Gremlin, and he met my car. He was not impressed.

But sometimes life takes a funny turn. The Gremlin didn't keep us apart. We got married and we could not afford to have two cars and I don't remember how or why but we ended up selling Ron's big boat of a car, and keeping my stubby one. To describe his humiliation in driving it would take yet another whole story.

14
I MET MY MATCH

I need to back up a bit to write about when I met Ron. My life with Ron began as a blind double-date with a mutual friend and his girlfriend one August a lifetime ago. When Ron and I met I thought: Nice guy. Handsome.

Recently, for our 50th wedding anniversary I bought a DVD of the movie we apparently saw on that date. (I just recently came across a calendar that I had kept for some reason and that was noted in it.) "Darling Lili" stars Rock Hudson and Julie Andrews, with music by Henry Mancini. It is an interesting movie. But did we remember any of it? Not one bit.

We had fun on that date and then we didn't go out again until a youth group banquet later in the fall. We figured out later that we had almost seen each other on Thanksgiving weekend near Hermon, Ontario. He was at Fraser Lake Camp with the Bethel youth group. I was at Frontier Forest (Frontier Boys' Camp at that time) on a staff retreat. I was in a truck that was having some mechanical problem and a car stopped to ask if they could help. I didn't see him in that car and he didn't see me in the back of the truck.

Later that fall we spent many evenings together in the "woodshed" after Ron was finished trucking for the day. Often he fell asleep on the couch. I opened a textbook to study or write a paper for one of my university courses. We did go out too, sometimes to Ron's church or to hear him sing in the Seiling/Martin quartet, and sometimes to St. Jacobs youth group where I was involved in leadership.

Our friendship did not involve a lot of getting to know each other by talking about our interests and values, or playing games, or going for walks, or any of the other methods of dating recommended in the daily Ann Landers columns. But somehow we had the confidence that we were meant to be together for the rest of our lives and in February we got engaged to be married, with the wedding planned for May. This is not a recommended way of doing courtship and I am thankful that none of our children followed our bizarre pattern.

The last semester of second year at university involved less studying than there should have been, and a whole lot of shopping for fabric, sewing my wedding dress, and helping Mom to refinish furniture for the Doddy house where we would be living. Grandpa and Grandma Horst had moved to Heritage House before this and their side of the house was vacant. Since Ron was working for

Home Hardware it was a handy spot to live, just minutes from the warehouse. Our wedding was at Conrad Grebel. Neutral ground. Simeon Hurst consented to marry us, and at the time we didn't know that later when we moved to the farm he would be our pastor at Bethel.

The first week of our honeymoon was spent travelling to northern Ontario and then spending the next weekend with the St. Jacobs youth at Frontier camp. Who does that on their honeymoon? Then back to our home we went, to be greeted as we walked down the hall by a sign saying the rent was due. My dad was having a bit of fun, but not as much fun as he and Mom had a little later after we were in bed and they chivareed us. Mom and Daddy liked my new husband, something I was always grateful for.

The second week of our life together was spent travelling in a Home Hardware truck to make deliveries to the stores in the Maritimes. That was the first of several trips that I made with Ron, and I can still feel the way my nose itched from the vibrations when I tried to sleep in the bunk.

Our early days of marriage were not without stress and it seems ironic that faith, in particular which church we attended, was the big stressor. It was an unwritten part of our marital agreement that we would attend the Pentecostal church. That was just how it was. The wife followed the husband to his church. Before our wedding this seemed quite doable, but it didn't last many months at all until I realised this was not going to work so well. Sensing some discontentment, the pastor started to visit me when Ron was away at work. Conversations got somewhat tangled when I felt pressure to practise my faith in ways that I was not accustomed to, and was told that speaking in tongues, specifically, would give evidence of whether I was a real Christian. I begged to differ. And although I argued that the greatest of all the gifts was love, I felt miserable. I tried and tried but in no way could I conjure up any unknown tongue, so I concluded I was not a good person. For sure not a good Christian. Although Ron was not present for these conversations he was upset by what I told him. It did not take us long to decide where we would not be going to church and it seemed a natural step to go to St. Jacobs Mennonite since that was where we lived and Ron had already become familiar with many of the people there. His parents were not at all pleased, but when we went to talk with them about it they didn't want to talk. It took quite a while before relations felt better. Even my pumpkin pie at the Thanksgiving meal I had prepared for them was a runny flop, and that's what I felt I was. Just a flop.

Another part of the unwritten marital agreement was that I would stay home, not working, and not going to school. That was okay for the first bit while I worked at Family and Children's Services in the summer and helped Mom and Daddy with gardening and picking the produce. But as winter came and there was less work and nothing to study, the novelty of my leisure time wore off.

Ron's parents had no grandchildren and especially Dolly was hoping that we could remedy that situation. More and more I warmed to that idea. When Rebecca was born on January 9th, 1973 she was the little girl that Dolly had always wanted and the recipient of much love and attention, along with a knitted pink sweater and bonnet set. It was the same set as the one she had knitted before each of her four boys was born. Rebecca received many knitted outfits, one for each birthday and sometimes in between.

15

LESSONS FROM MY PARENTS

Living in the Doddy house those first three years of our married life was a special time, a privilege. Sure, I had lived with my parents all my life before marriage but living with them as an adult, married and anticipating having a family of our own, had a new feel. I paid attention to their relationship in a different way, and I thought about how they parented me. It was good preparation for shaping us as parents.

It has often been said that there really should be more preparation or some great book to teach us how to raise our children. And while there is a plethora of books that attempt to do just that, it seems to me that there are many tips to be gained just by watching others.

What I learned from my parents was usually by observation. Most was caught, not taught. My parents were not preachy, but by watching and listening to comments about someone else's behaviour I was quite able to discern the path I should be taking. Mom was soft on instruction or reprimand, and Daddy could change my behaviour with just a look or perhaps a "Chee Willickers" said quietly under his breath. These were the days of "children are to be seen and not heard" and "spare the rod, spoil the child" but, gladly, my sensitive spirit and my inherent need to please helped me, for the most part, to avoid punishment.

I learned at a very early age that we all helped with the work. With a large garden and acres of potatoes to be harvested there was not a lack of opportunity to pitch in and help. I remember picking strawberries with my sister as she taught me some rhymes and arithmetic skills. After helping to pick the cucumbers, my work was not over because that mountain of cukes needed to be sorted into baskets of varying sizes - some for gherkins, some for dills, and then the big ones to grind up for relish. I think there were 5 or 6 different sizes. Some customers were very particular about the size of the cucumbers so I tried my best to please. Later I graduated to the potato field, and was then under Daddy's tutelage.

I would be remiss to mention only the outdoor jobs. In them I found enjoyment, but not so much with the indoor ones. Although I now enjoy handwashing dishes as a lavender-scented, calming experience, this was not the case in my earlier years. Perhaps it was the dish soap.

I learned to order my day. Not in a Benedictine way, but in my dad's way. I watched as he tended his property with great pride. He encouraged and helped Mom each summer to plant the flower beds with the reddest of geraniums, and mowed the lawn like clockwork each Saturday. The car was washed each Sunday morning. Often, at lunchtime, the cash box was taken out, contents spread on the bed and counted. He kept his cards close to his chest. He sat at the table at 12 noon and at 6 o'clock supper and expected the meal to be served, and was seldom disappointed. Before retiring in the evening he made a tour of the property to see what required some work, and then he would do the very same thing again in the morning. There was a certain order to things and everything went more smoothly if that order was not interrupted.

I like order and I find myself attempting to bring order to my life, but it sometimes seems that I have only gotten as far as putting my shoes in a straight line when I come in from the out-of-doors. And that I learned from the Benedictines.

I learned whatever patience I have from Mom. She was a very patient wife. She was a patient mother. She was a patient aunt when her sister needed some summer relief from six children in a small log cabin in the north. She was a patient grandmother, taking time for visits from her grandchildren even when she was busy.

I learned the importance of faith. Daddy faithfully attended Sunday morning and evening services and any special meetings, but drew the line at small group discussions. His strict punctuality had him at the church early, sometimes half an hour early. Mom didn't always go to evening meetings, but she demonstrated her faith by being a girls' club leader, and by making floral arrangements for the front of the church. She donated several paintings for the Mennonite Central Committee Relief Sale, to aid people around the world.

We didn't have a lot of personal chats about faith but often had "preacher for Sunday dinner" and in that way I was able to hear what was important to them in their faith.

I observed generosity as I saw my parents sharing with others by tithing, giving food, giving time. When I think back to their busy lives, especially during the summer, they still made time for conversation with customers, some of whom became good friends. I remember, as well, their generosity with some neighbours and family who needed a helping hand.

Mom and Daddy's 50th Wedding Anniversary

I was taught the value of on-going learning with the availability of the Encyclopedia and a large Webster's dictionary that I was urged to consult when Daddy used a word that he had just read in one of the books from his towering stack.

I learned that one needn't talk on the phone for more than five minutes, and the water in the bathtub should at the most be two inches deep.

I absorbed the importance of family as I was a part of the gatherings that happened annually with the Horst family. I discovered my roots and the importance of having strong roots to grow strong branches - the mature "branches" that I now delight in learning from, and the fun and wonderful younger "sprouts and twigs and branches" that are growing.

16
PRACTICAL ADVICE FROM MY MOTHER

Mom wasn't one to give a lot of advice. No "you should do this" or "oh no, you shouldn't do that." The shoulds in my life, those things that later in life send people into therapy sessions to rid themselves of guilt and shame, did not come from her. If there were shoulds, they were self-inflicted by my overly active, sensitive nature.

That is not to say that Mom had no opinion or advice to give, but that it was usually not verbal. Her advice sometimes came by example or by affirming what I was doing right, and then I was left to examine my actions for what she didn't affirm and try to do a self-correction. I often picked up on nonverbal cues — a look or a sigh or a *tsk*, although even those were more likely to come from Daddy than from Mom. And, as I have said before, I was a pleaser so I would do whatever I could to make things feel better.

But that makes me sound like a perennially pleasant, compliant person, which I wasn't. In retrospect, I can think of situations in which I could have used some advice, and maybe at times some sharp advice. I feel ashamed over the times I slipped out the door after a meal instead of helping with the dishes, or perhaps neglected to clean my room. Or I think of when Ron and I were dating and the goodbyes got too long, or were perhaps too late. There would be this "ahem" clearing of the throat or a bit of rustling about in their bedroom. Clear signals that it was time that we end our visit so Mom could get back to sleep.

Emerson's bush at sap boiling time.

And one time, in my graying years, when I had tried solving the problem with the help of a "natural" colouring that over several weeks turned my hair kinda reddish, she hesitantly approached the conundrum with "Now I don't want to hurt your feelings but...". I took her signal and ever after that I let my hairdresser look after my aging tresses.

There were other bits of sage advice, ones that stuck. Like the time when I was quite young and she called, "Jeanette, come here! See?" upon which I did come and see two cats that seemed to be in a bit of a tussle on the grass outside the picture window. With no follow up explanation, it was quite confusing until years later when I read some of Linda's nursing school textbooks and filled in the missing blanks of my sex education.

When I had graduated from ironing handkerchiefs and tea towels to pressing Daddy's shirts, Mom gave me specific instructions saying, "This is how Mrs Henderson told me to do it," implying that was the proper way. Mom was a maid for Mrs Henderson and that lady remains in residence in a back corner of my mind, whispering her bits of practical wisdom.

When I wanted to watch a summer evening baseball game in the park at the other end of town and Mom knew it would be dark when I walked home, her advice was to carry a sharp hat pin. But, why? Well, that was so I could give a good poke at anyone who crept up behind me. I almost think she told me to aim for his eye, but that couldn't be. My sweet and gentle mother had a mean streak in her?

Then, in my early homemaking days, when I asked for further instructions on the method for a recipe she had given to me, in response she said, "Oh, just do it how you think." But that was the point: I didn't know how to think about it.

And the one I love the very best: When the children were young and there was so much to do that I couldn't keep up with tending the flower beds, Mom wisely said, "Don't worry about the flower beds now. Your flowers are growing in the house." Funny thing. My house flowers are all grown up now but the weeding in my gardens is still a challenge.

Some days I wish that I had asked for more of Mom's advice. I think she probably had a storehouse from which she could have drawn if I had only asked. And that may have given her the same feeling of honour I experience when my children come for advice from me.

17
IT'S IN THE GENES

"Oh, you look so much like your mother." That is a remark I have often heard, especially since I let my hair go "au naturel." Mom had curly hair that she wore in a French roll for most of my growing up years. Later she had it cut, with my father's blessing, and then when her hair was able to have the freedom to do its own thing it got curly, though never again like her grade school pictures when her head was just a mass of unruly curls. So cute.

My hair is like Mom's, but in some ways our looks were not

alike. Mom had hazel eyes and I have the dark brown Horst eyes. Mom was short, probably no more than 5 feet 2 or 3 inches on a good day and I have been 5 feet 8 inches since about grade ten. Probably I got my height from the Horst side of the family because the Sniders are all shorter. For most of his life Daddy was six feet tall. People have also remarked that I look like my dad because I have "that Horst look." I'm not sure if that's good or bad. And I have been told that my humour is similar - "Oh, that sounded just like Uncle Dave." And I'm not sure if that is good or bad.

Mom was very crafty. She was an accomplished sewer, made wonderful flower gardens, was a great cook, braided mats, pieced quilts, embroidered, collected antiques before that was popular and then refinished the furniture, and most of all she was an artist painting many, many landscapes. I am grateful that I had the opportunity to see Mom do all these things because in watching her I learned some of her skills. One thing I didn't learn from her was cooking. Her kitchen was tiny and she always said there was no room for anyone else, unless they were doing the dishes. But although she didn't share her kitchen, she did share recipes that I still enjoy.

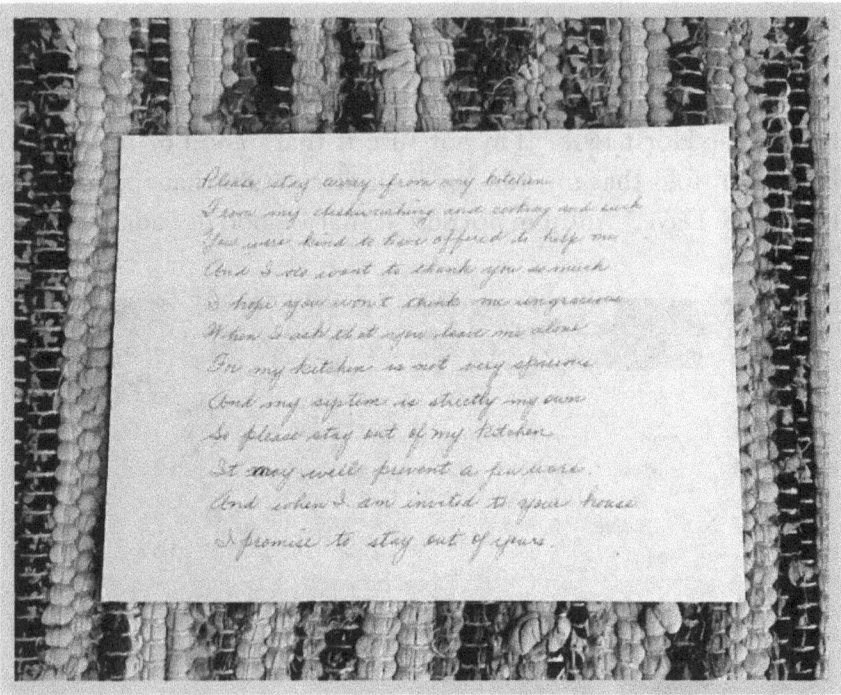

Daddy was a reader. Most nights he read before going to sleep and, during the slower times, in his lazy boy at the living room bay window, he revelled in his magazines and books, especially those about the "Civil Wahh." It was from his extensive reading that he learned words not commonly used and when he tried out one of these newfound words in conversation he would say it a couple of times and then spell it. I share his love of reading, but my genres of choice are a bit different. And I do at times find myself at least tempted to spell a word I have used, and often now when words and names elude me I substitute a word or name, knowing full well it is not right. Just like my dad.

Mom and Daddy shared a love of watching wrestling on TV and got quite animated about it. In those first years when Ron and I were living in the Doddy house and had people over, we sometimes needed to explain the sudden outbursts coming from my parents' house. I never got bitten by that wrestling bug. Ditto on the Honeymooners and Archie Bunker. Their choice of programming often surprised me, for the gentle people they were - well, Mom at least. My choice of TV viewing might not be better, just different.

They lived frugally in their early marriage and Daddy was always careful with money. He held the purse strings and Mom knew very little about their finances, except that the money that she invested from the sale of her oil paintings in the early years of mutual fund investing stood them in good stead in their later years. Mom was like many other women of her age who knew little about finances, and a big part of my decision to work at the Mennonite Savings and Credit Union was to educate myself in money matters.

I observed my parents' actions of generosity to others, by helping out financially or baking a pie or sewing clothing for newcomers to Canada or family members that needed a lift. Today those acts encourage me to live more open-handedly.

Daddy was an introvert. A loner, he would say. He was most comfortable on his home turf, on his terms. I also love to be at home. I love to travel, to see other places and meet other people, but then I am soon homesick for my place and my people. With his produce business Daddy was constantly interrupted to tend the garden stand. He welcomed most interruptions because it was his livelihood, but it was quite evident when he had reached his quota of customers for the day or the season and was ready to be alone with his thoughts or his garden. I recognize within myself that same need for solitude.

His love of nature in general and gardening in particular are things I share with him. While travelling he would marvel at the scenery and in the potato field at times he broke into a hymn of praise, sung above the noise of the tractor and potato digger. Each morning, and most evenings during the growing season, he would make the rounds of the property, assessing how things were doing and what needed tending. I enjoy morning rounds, if not physically, then mentally, to order my days, and at those moments when life couldn't possibly feel better I go to the piano and sing my hymn of praise.

On days when our farm seems like Grand Central Station with people coming for their stored vehicles or guys coming to talk about hunting or just to talk and I am ready to lock the gate at the end of our lane, I am reminded of Mom's patience in all those years of serving customers, often while her potatoes were cooking and beginning to burn. Aunt Naomi told me about a time when Mom was heating some wax on the stove and was called out to tend to some customer's needs. When she came back into the house there was a cloud of smoke and the walls were black. She said that day Mom did some very fast scrubbing before Daddy came in for lunch.

In many ways Mom had great patience to which I can only aspire. She was a submissive wife, like the church taught. Sometimes when I think back to Mom's final years when she was getting more and more tired, I wonder if she may have needed to assert

IT'S IN THE GENES

herself for her own wellbeing, but that was not her way. Now, in more recent years, things are slowly changing and women are finding their own voice. I am a fledgling at asserting myself, but I am realizing the benefits of being a stronger woman. The slogan I have adopted since my seventieth birthday is that I want "the rest of my life to be the best of my life" and that might involve asserting myself in ways and at times that Mom would not have considered.

And so it seems that much is in the genes. I am a mix of Elva and David, my mom and my dad, shaped and formed by their lives and values and beliefs; the cord of faith-nature-family, weaving through and around my life.

❦ 18 ❧
A RANDOM ACT OF KINDNESS

The early years of our marriage were lean years for Ron and me. While some people have the common sense to discuss money matters before the nuptials, we did not broach that conversation. After all, love is blind, as they say, so what did finances have to do with anything? I could have taken a clue about the state of affairs from the fact that Ron didn't have enough money to buy me a present that Christmas before we were married but, like I said, my head was in the clouds.

So I was surprised when Mom approached me one day with the offer of a shopping trip to buy a new "Sunday" winter coat. I have no memory of the coat I had been wearing, only that Mom deemed it necessary that I have a new one. It was not my birthday or any other special day and in those years we didn't officially have Random Act of Kindness days, but this was definitely a random act of kindness.

Mom and I browsed several stores in downtown Kitchener. This was before the days of shopping malls, of course, but we had our favourite clothing stores - Goudies, Eatons, Budds, Woolworths, and maybe more that I don't remember. I do remember that I tried on coats at several stores, and finally settled on a brown tweed belted coat that I wore for years.

That coat still hangs in the closet. I can't part with it. It has a classic look that could be dressed up or down. It could be shortened for more casual wear. It could be cut into strips for a lovely braided mat, and I might do that when I get old. But for now, as for many years, it lives in a plastic clothing bag on the very left side of the front closet. It is a reminder of kindness shown to me.

In many other ways I have been a recipient of kindness - gifts from my children or grandchildren, a jar of homemade cream cheese from a neighbour, a quilt from another neighbour, a blessing from an older woman at a mosque in Turkey, after I helped her down the steps, tickets for a concert, meals brought in when we lived in a trailer on the barn hill, after our fire.

Many times I have been blessed with kindness. Reminders to "pass-it-on."

19
LEARNING FROM MY GRANDPARENTS

As I had more time with my parents I learned more about my grandparents.

I knew my Grandma and Grandpa Horst well because for all my growing-up years they lived in the Doddy house attached to our family's home. They were only one door away whenever I wanted to play a game or talk or wind their clock at the same time every Saturday night. I had the unique opportunity to observe them on a day-to-day basis. I saw them as they lived together, always working side by side, especially in the kitchen. I have Grandma's 5-year diary in which she notes their daily events. She writes, "We made Brown Betty", "We cleaned the upstairs room", "We washed and ironed some...". We, always we. In their last years they were separated for a few days while Grandpa was in hospital. After he returned to Heritage House and their shared room, a nurse saw them snuggled together in one of their single beds. That strong bond of togetherness remained even though both, by that time, were in deep dementia. Always "we". As a newlywed that left a strong impression. That's what I wanted our marriage and our family to be like.

My maternal grandma I saw less frequently, but I still had a connection with her. At least one Sunday afternoon a month my mom, dad, and I — and after I got my driver's licence it would often be just Mom and I — would travel to Kitchener or Fairview Home in Preston (Cambridge) to visit with her. I was always mesmerized by her hooked rugs, her quilt patches, her knitted corncob potholders, and other projects, usually piled on top of a jigsaw puzzle in progress on top of her card table. Her hands were always busy.

Grandma Knarr's first husband, Elias Snider, was a man that I wish I had had a chance to know. He died when my mother was the tender age of twelve so her memories of those early years with him were all she was left with.

To know the kind of man he was I asked my mother, and then later Aunt Naomi and Aunt Olive. They all mention him in their life stories, each from their own perspective. Through their descriptions of family life when they were young, they weave stories of family times together having picnics down by the river, or Sunday afternoon drives in their 1917 Ford touring car to places like

Puslinch Lake, Forks of the Credit, or Aldershot (near Hamilton) where relatives had a melon farm, or just staying at home playing family games in the evening. I got a sense of a well-loved, family-oriented father and I can imagine Elias as a warm and friendly grandfather.

Grandpa Snider had many heart-breaking experiences — the death of his first wife, and then his second wife and child in childbirth, the barn burning, and a severe hail storm one year that caused him to lose the whole crop. Mom once wrote that his spirits became low and he struggled with depression, just like the world that was heading into the years of the Great Depression.

There are few photos of him, but in a close-up of Grandma and Elias together, unsmiling, which was the manner for pictures in those days, he appears to be a kind, tender-hearted, perhaps sensitive person. The photo was taken in their good years before the fire, the hail, the poverty, and the illness. The eyes are gentle, without revealing the pain that Elias suffered from severe headaches and Bright's Disease (chronic inflammation of the kidneys). Aunt Olive said that she remembered so well the morning that he died. He had called the children into the room. "Naomi and Breton sat on the bed and Elva, Alice and I were crying. He told us not to cry - that everything is alright. Edna and Rheta did not get home in time and he passed away a few minutes before they arrived."

I wish that I could have known Grandpa Snider, but I am grateful that I experience(d) his gentle spirit that has passed on to his children.

For my grandparents, times were different than they are now. Life was, at times, a day-to-day struggle, but they made the best of it that they could. When I have days that challenge me, I draw courage and strength from their inherent values, faith, and perseverance.

20
READY FOR CHILDREN?

In anticipation of our first child, I made my first quilt — a train, embroidered on white fabric, bordered with soft yellow. Dolly, Mom, and I were quilting that crib quilt when I realized it was time to head off to the hospital.

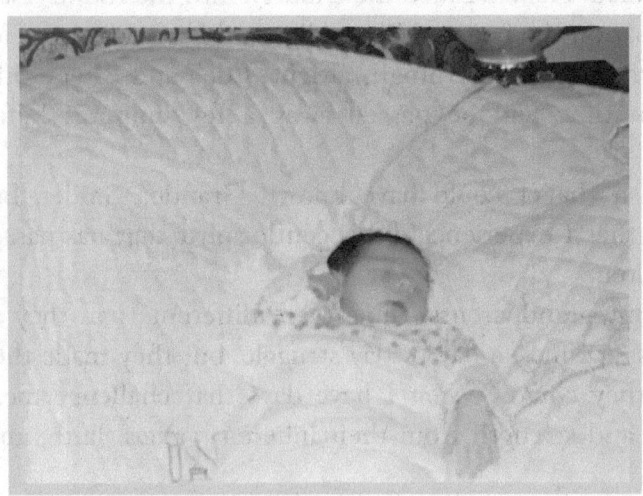

It was a rather new thing at the time to allow the husbands to be present for the delivery, but Ron was eager to be there. He did well, though the medical staff were a bit concerned. Through the fog of pain, I heard them ask a few times, "How is father doing? Is he going to be okay?" He managed, and was, in the end, game to repeat being present in the delivery room three more times.

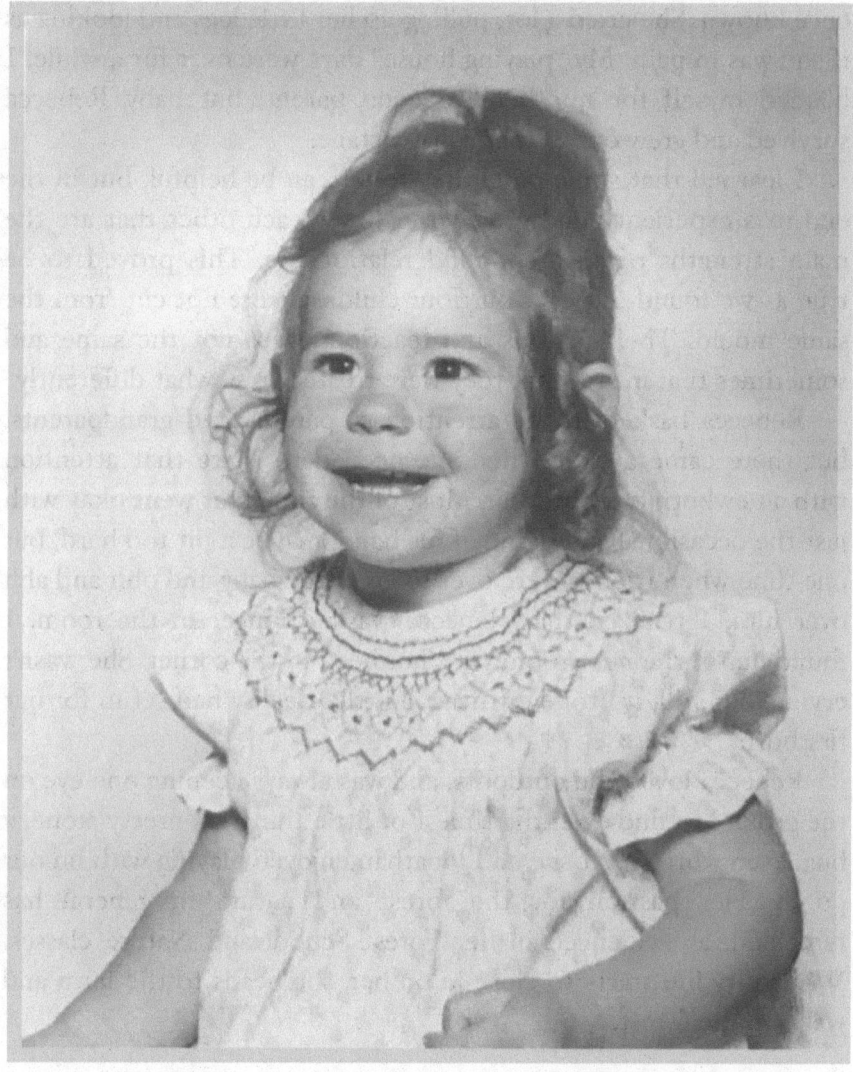

We were delighted with our little newborn. We named her Rebecca Jane because we liked the name Rebecca and the baby naming book said that names should be of different lengths so our baby had a 3-syllable, a 1-syllable and a 2-syllable name. After initially being confused about day and night and that we sleep at night, she basically just ate and slept. Mom said it was like we were playing house. Then, around three weeks of age, she made her presence known. She cried a lot, pulling up her little legs and looking as if she was in pain. My "playing house" days were over for a while. I blamed myself for not being a good parent, but baby Rebecca survived and grew out of that colicky stage.

I learned that some parenting books can be helpful, but in the end it is experience and growing to know each other that are the main strengths of a parent/child relationship. This proved to be true as we found out that our four children were not cut from the same mould. Their actions and reactions were not the same and sometimes that meant that they were treated somewhat differently.

Rebecca basked in the attention of parents and grandparents, but there came a time when she needed to share that attention with a newborn baby brother. Most of the time that went okay with just the occasional squeezing of his hand, maybe a bit too hard, but one time when friends were over to greet the baby and ohh and ahh over him, I realized that Rebecca was no longer in the room. I found her in the next room with her head in the corner. She wasn't crying, but still, it broke my heart a little. Reality had set in for our firstborn.

Rebecca loved the outdoors, and was always keeping one eye on the ground to find even the tiniest of little things. A pretty stone, a bug, even worms that she and Jonathan enjoyed playing with on our porch. Her passion for the forest and nature in general has remained, as evidenced in her Forest School and Nature classes. When city life starts to close in on her, she heads to the farm and walks in the forest.

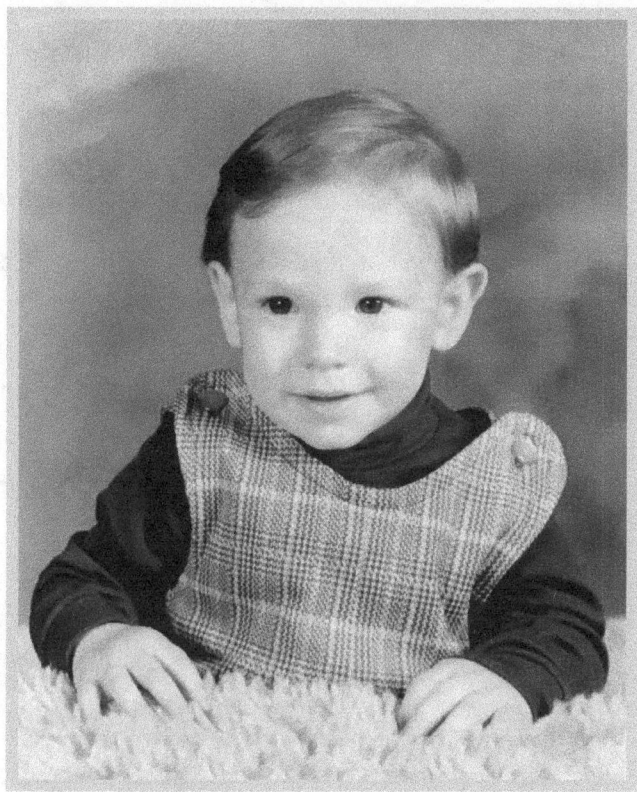

Jonathan Ronald was born May 6, 1975. He seemed inquisitive and eager to face the world from the moment he could open his eyes and look around. Like his sister before him, he had dark curly hair, but had a more robust build. He was a contented baby. In another part of the book, I tell the story of his stay in the hospital at just over three weeks of age.

Jonathan's curiosity about all things remained with him. He was usually eager to go places and do things, and then just as eager to move on to the next thing. At convocation, when he was introduced to give the valedictorian speech, he was described as a Renaissance man. Perhaps in his earlier years he might have been called a Renaissance boy, interested in many things.

Rebecca was already in school and Jonathan was wishing he could go, but at four was not old enough, when we had another boy.

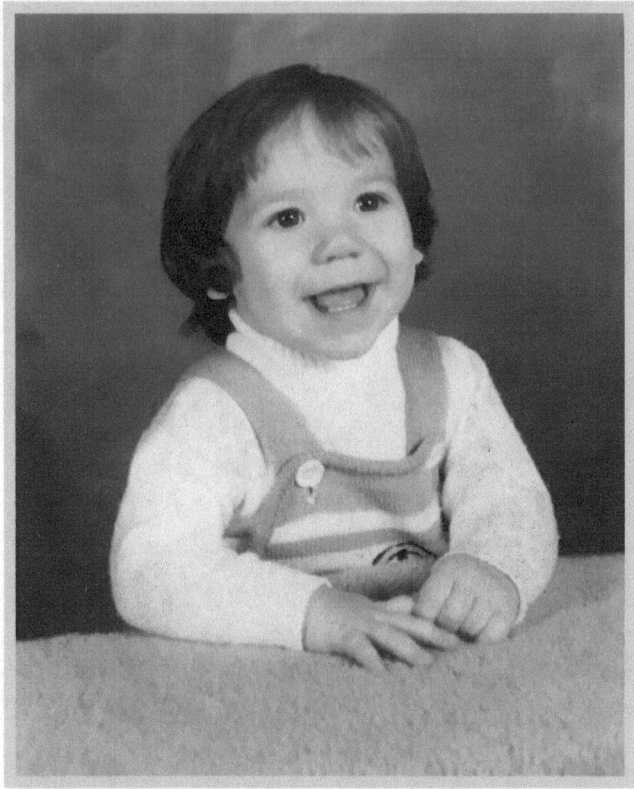

David Horst was born October 19, 1979 - our International Year of the Child project, we joked. He was a dark-haired, chubby little guy. He wasn't born with rubber boots on, but from the time he could crawl, and then walk, he wore rubber boots and drove his Fisher-Price truck around the kitchen and then later up and down the laneway in front of the house. He had a shorter, muscled body that wanted to be on the go, except when he watched Sesame Street or later, "Dacks a Huzzart" (Dukes of Hazzard). He developed his own basic language, something we almost missed after he learned to talk like the rest of us.

David had an appealing charm as a little boy. That charm, coupled with energy to make things happen, now bodes well in his role as a project manager, working closely with his clients.

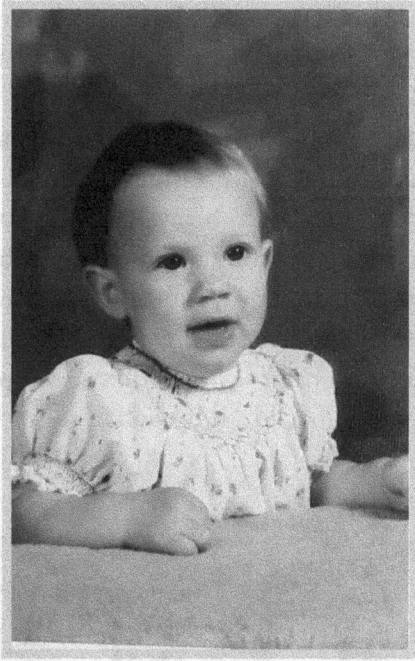

Ron and I had talked about adopting a fourth child, a baby girl. I think it was my days with Family and Children's Services that had steered me in that direction. But God had different plans for our family and on August 22, 1981 we welcomed Bethany Danielle. This little baby girl surprised us. She didn't have lots of black, curly hair like her siblings, but instead she had just a few short wisps of blond hair, lighter skin tone, and hazel eyes like her grandma Horst. From the first night home, Bethany seemed to know that nighttime was for sleeping, and until she was teething she gave her parents good, long hours of rest. I learned that I didn't have to wake her up to see if she was okay. A great gift of sleep for a busy mom. As a toddler she loved books. When she was put into her crib for her nap she had a couple of stuffed toys, and a big pile of books. That passion for reading continues in her children.

Bethany, as the youngest, sometimes had siblings talking for her, but that didn't mean she had no voice or was without a sense of adventure. She could do things for herself, as she proved when she left to spend a year in Germany, with the Intermenno program. The day we dropped her off at the airport I cried on our return home. My youngest had flown the coop!

They were busy years of trying to raise our children in the best way we could while running our business (Ronald Seiling Trucking) too. Many times Ron needed to be away when he was long-distance trucking and I learned how to manage things at home. I can think of many times when I didn't do the best parenting, but somehow we survived. When I watch our children now and see the adults they have become, with their own children, I am proud to see them contributing and giving back to life, each in their own way.

21

LETTING GO

May 2020 was a month when the temperature soared to the 30s on some days, and one week we apparently broke the record set in May 1975. And it struck me that it was this same week 45 years ago that Ron and I took our little baby boy to hospital, the same hospital where he had been born just three weeks earlier. The nurses took him and stripped him of everything — his blanket, his sleeper, his diaper — and immediately inserted the IV. His fever had spiked and they were going to run tests to ascertain the cause.

At that time there were no accommodations for parents to stay with their child so they sent us home to rest. Driving home I had only a little pile of clothes in my lap where my baby should have laid. At the stop sign in Conestogo, I watched my cousin and her then-boyfriend drive by, laughing together. I remember wondering how they could be laughing when I was in such deep pain.

Although my mind could not comprehend how I could go on, I needed to go on because we had our two and a half year old Rebecca who needed us to be there for her too. I determined I must be brave for her as well as for this little life that had only just begun.

Jonathan had been born on May 6th, 1975, within a short time after our speedy police escort to the hospital. Delivery went quickly. I remember that when I first held him, he pushed away from my chest with his strong arms, and through blinking eyes he looked around at his new world. He was an "easy" baby who seldom cried. Those were busy times with a new baby, and keeping up with a toddler, and the weeds in the garden, and the trucking business. All had seemed well, and when Jonathan seemed to be quite warm I, at first, tried to dismiss it as being because of the hot weather we were having. But my concern did not go away. Some people had been visiting to see this new baby, and as soon as they left we headed to the hospital.

There were tests done, but nothing showed up as a cause. The fever remained high. I would go to the hospital as soon as I could in the morning, and stay as long as I could in the evening. I wanted him to have breastmilk as often as he could, but there was a day when he needed to be on clear fluids for a procedure. I remember wearing sunglasses most of the time, especially when I stopped in at Mom and Daddy's. I didn't take off my sunglasses because they would have seen my eyes, red from crying. We were not a huggy family and that day was no different. A hug may have opened a floodgate of emotions and I needed to "keep it together" and carry on.

I don't clearly recall, but I think it was the fourth day, and the doctor and pediatrician still did not know what was causing the fever. I remember praying a lot and realizing that I must release my strong hold on this little boy. My Sunday School teachings over many years had taught me that much. I thought I had already been as brave as I could be, but this took my bravery to a whole new level.

And then Simeon and Edna Hurst visited. Simeon was the pastor at Bethel Mennonite Church at that time and was doing his pastoral duty, but he also had married us, and was a relative and a friend. They prayed for Jonathan. It was very soon after that the fever went down. And very soon we took our little boy back home where he belonged.

They gave it a name. They said maybe it was a urinary tract infection.

We had given our little boy the name Jonathan which means "gift from God". I had released him back to God, and then God gave our gift back to us.

Parenting is not without challenges. Ultimately our children are gifts from God, and we are privileged to love and nurture them.

22
PARENTING

For many people a star-studded career is a great achievement, but for me one of the greatest achievements of my life is raising my "brood" of four.

Maple syrup on snow — taffy-pulling

I watch them with eyes of wonder and pride, puzzling that they were, in fact, each born and raised under the shelter of this humble 1850s house, grew roots in the fields and forest of this Eighth Line of Pilkington Township, and then flew to other parts, some near, some farther away. It isn't an achievement that's solely mine but one shared with Ron, their grandparents, mentors along the way, and guidance from above for the tough parts that came along in the challenges of raising a family.

International Plowing Match 1984 in Teviotdale

I have often pondered that we didn't have a guidebook, and we felt quite ill-equipped to raise these young lives. (Sorry Dr Spock, but sometimes your advice just didn't cut it.) Along the way, it seemed, life itself became the guide. And if I were graded, I most surely would not have achieved all A's for my decisions in parenting; sometimes barely a passing grade. But somehow crooked paths became straight, and I couldn't be more proud of the person each of them has become.

An achievement is defined as "a thing done successfully, typically by effort, courage, and skill." Raising children takes a lot of courage and much effort. The skills seem to come with practising. Their fruitful lives are the reward.

"...*as a hen gathereth her chicks under her wings*..."

Thanks be to God.

23
WORK

Work started for me at an early age, when I didn't know it was work. I was simply joining my family in what needed to be done in the garden and in the potato field. It was mostly fun because my parents were my "bosses" and they did not believe in child labour. I don't think that I got paid for the garden work. That was expected as part of being a busy family. For the work in the potato field, as I grew older, I was often paid on the same schedule as the boys that worked for Daddy, but not at the same rate.

I think I could pick as fast as they could, and when I was older I could schlepp full bushels with the best of them, but Daddy had a different pay scale for me. I was paid less per hour because I got room and board and perhaps also because I was a girl, although I am not certain. In the potato field I worked hard, but as the boss Daddy made it fun, and treated us well.

In my later teen years, I worked at the Mill End Store downtown. My aunt Olive worked there and perhaps she had gotten that job for me. She was familiar with my work ethic because I had worked for her in the kitchen one summer at Pioneer Girls' Camp.

Working at the store was my first job in customer service, aside from serving customers at my parents' roadside produce stand. At first I was a bit nervous, but before long I enjoyed the variety of jobs - measuring yardage, perhaps for three dozen flannelette diapers for an expected new baby; finding the right size of boots for a young boy; rooting to the bottom of the towel end box to search for another blue towel to match what the customer had. The adding machine and cash register and balancing at the end of the day were new learnings too. What I hadn't anticipated was the variety of people and character traits that would walk through the door. It was a real study in human nature, and good fodder for stories at the supper table after I returned home for the day.

For two summers I worked at Frontier Boys' Camp near Fraser Lake. The first summer I was a kitchen boy and pony girl. The second summer I was promoted to camp mother. For an 18-year-old that was a bit of a stretch, but it was a good experience. The boys were from 8 to 14 years of age, and all had been in trouble with the law for one thing or another. I had a little 8-year-old boy tell me about his B&E's. I needed to ask what a B&E was - Break and Enter, of course, but my small town mind could not imagine how this was possible. Another, perhaps 10-year-old, told me about when he had hotwired a car and taken it for a joyride in Toronto. Staff had long, action-packed days, and then stayed up to write reports and socialize at night. To say the least, I learned a lot those summers. And I loved it.

Near the end of my second year of university I got a lead from the man for whom I babysat. He said there was a summer opening at Guelph Family and Children's Services, to assist in the children's services area. After a short interview with a straight-backed, chain-smoking, very proper, older lady, I was offered the job. I worked with Marnie and the newborn and younger children, and Pat and the older children. I was tickled to have my own office.

The work was varied. My first job was to take a bunch of supplies from the closet and make up layettes for the babies that CAS (Children's Aid Society) picked up from the hospital to take to foster homes. I met with Marnie and Pat to go over some of the things I would be doing. They were both very busy so I was often left on my own, once they knew I was okay to manage independently.

In my role, I picked up children from their foster homes and took them to doctor's appointments, and sometimes that involved driving to SickKids Hospital in Toronto. When I reflect on that now, I am amazed that as a just-turned-20-year-old I had the nerve to drive into the belly of Toronto, and manage the traffic flow there. Probably the streets were not as busy as they are today.

There were other trips, as well, to Windsor for appointments, and to northern Ontario to drop off campers, and to many fostering homes across the county of Wellington.

A few times, I went to the Guelph General Hospital to pick up a newborn who was going to spend time, until adopted, in a foster home. I didn't attend court cases but one time I was asked to visit a foster home to examine a toddler for sexual abuse. I was quite innocent and not even certain what I was looking for. It was a different world, and I was learning a lot.

In my second summer with CAS, I was given more responsibility with my own caseload, and before I left at the end of August I was offered a position as a full-time social worker with them, despite the fact that I had no degree. However, by that time, I was pregnant with a baby scheduled to arrive in January. I declined the offer.

During those two summers of working in the world of social work I received a valuable education. It opened my eyes to a world different from the sheltered life of my childhood. It was practical knowledge, more valuable than textbooks could have offered.

Within a few years of our life together, Ron's dad decided to sell the farm that he had bought ten years before. It was the farm on which Ron and his brothers had honed their farming skills. Ron had already started a fledgling gravel trucking business and was interested in buying the farm.

That was the one move I have had in my life.

It had been a unique time for all of us when Ron and I, and then Rebecca, lived in the Doddy house and were able to be back and forth with Mom and Daddy at any time. Little Rebecca took full advantage of being able to just push open the adjoining door and meet Grandpa and Grandma, still at their breakfast table, and share a grapefruit with them. Probably with Grandma because Grandpa was not into sharing food with anyone, not even his little granddaughter. Mom said that she cried when we drove out the driveway, headed to our new home.

Our farmhouse needed some work so we were busy with that for a while, and then Ron dove more seriously into the gravel business. Some parts of the business involved me at different times. I took phone orders for gravel from farmers who thought I should know where the 3rd and the 12th and all those other roads were. Luckily, when I radioed the truckers, they seemed to know exactly where to go. The radio frequency was shared with a taxi company from Windsor so I needed to tune out all that to be sure to hear when it was one of the truckers needing something or other. And this all happened in our kitchen as I tried to do the housework and tend to our toddler and new baby. I also tried to quickly learn how to do payroll and billing and banking and weighing truckloads at times. I was very glad when Grand Central Station for the business moved from our kitchen to the scalehouse across the field on the new pit lane. The truck traffic rumbled back and forth on the pit lane, and not just outside our kitchen window. We hired our neighbour, Henry, to sit in the scalehouse and weigh the trucks. This was progress.

Fast forward a few years and more babies, and a change in our business. We were no longer running the business ourselves, but had leased the pit to The Murray Group. Ron was back to trucking, and I was freed up from most of the participation with the gravel business. Mind you, I worked, at times, as a flag person and also found myself back in the scalehouse, weighing trucks for truckers with strange comments, but for the most part I was freed up for other things.

I volunteered at Salem Public School often enough that the principal once commented that I spent more time there than he did. Bethany was a preschooler at the time and went with me to help in the school library and for a long time, when asked what she was going to do when she was older, she answered that she wanted to be a library helper. That aspiration was strengthened when, many years later, she got her masters degree in Library Sciences.

Volunteering led to a part-time, sometimes supply, job with a class of children with special needs at Salem, and later at Drayton Public School. I loved that work and have often wondered about some of those special children. Some I know have passed on, others I still wonder about. Sometimes the work was difficult when trying to open up windows in the child's life where they seemed to be locked tight. And sometimes I learned life lessons that only they could teach me.

Later, on a whim, I applied for a Member Service Representative position at Elmira Mennonite Savings and Credit Union. I thought I should increase my knowledge of dollars and cents. I was offered the position and I ended up staying on for thirteen years, some of those working strictly in investments.

At that point perhaps I would have had the opportunity to start a different career. But a door didn't close, and a window didn't open.

After Bethany had been in school for a few years, I asked her what she would like to be when she grew up. She immediately countered with, "I don't know, what do you want to be when you grow up?"

As it turned out, I did not have a clear career path. While Ron was away many times with his trucking jobs, my "job" was being at home with the children. And that was a privilege.

A quote by Joseph Campbell recently popped off the newspaper page at me, "*The privilege of a lifetime is being who you are.*" I can relate to that. I do not regret that I cannot refer back to a big, illustrious career. I found worth in meeting the small need where my passion met that need. I feel that I have had a lifetime of being who I am, and it has been a privilege.

24
PUMPKIN PEOPLE

Some work is more like play, and that was the case with Mom and Daddy's Fall Pumpkin People display. It was something that began on a whim and eventually grew as an attraction to the point that it became a traffic hazard and had to be ended for safety reasons.

In the fall of 1970 Mom had phlebitis and needed to stay inside with her leg elevated. Under those restrictions, thoughts had an opportunity to wander and eventually landed on a memory of their trip to Pennsylvania. On a country road they had noticed a garden produce stand and as they looked more closely, they saw Pumpkin People made from pumpkins and squash. This tickled Mom's imagination and she wondered if they could replicate that. Mom described what they had seen as best she could and then directed the process from her lazy boy at the living room bay window. Thus began a tradition that lasted close to 20 years.

That first year the pumpkins and squash grew in a manner such that we could fashion the "people" totally with vegetables. The pumpkins were the head and body, and the butternut squash had grown with long, curved necks, perfect for shaping arms and legs.

In subsequent years when the garden produce did not grow in that way, we needed to start dressing up the Pumpkin People.

One special display that we made was in 1987, for my parents' 50th wedding anniversary. That year the cornstalk horses pulled a wagon with a top on and a pretty spiffy couple, dressed in full regalia and riding in style.

We had a lot of fun, often laughing when a character we had created turned out looking like someone we knew, or someone we would like to know. The guy in the outhouse caused some giggles, and also some concern for me at times when I would come around the corner and think "Oh, no! There's my dad forgetting to close the door and sitting in there for all the world to see!" We often used Daddy's old plaid shirts and denim overalls to dress them up and sometimes at a glance Daddy was hard to pick out in that motley crew of Fall visitors. The Pumpkin People grew in numbers every year, spreading out in different areas of their property.

Many people returned annually to visit and some suggested to my parents that they should put out a donation box. After some thought we made up a sign, cut a hole in an old cream can, chose a charity to help the homeless on the streets of Toronto, and then we were awed by the very generous donations of visitors.

As the Fall Pumpkin People tradition continued to grow, there was a downside to it. On weekends cars, and sometimes tour buses, lined the street on both sides for people to come and see the attraction. Neighbours were getting frustrated and it was becoming unsafe for traffic. I created the display at our farm for a couple more years, providing a fun activity for some school tours, but eventually that too came to an end. Sometimes, now as the October winds blow and the colours start to turn, I see Pumpkin People that others have made. That gives me joy and I think back to the long tradition of Mom, Daddy and me working (or maybe it was playing?) together, making memories.

25
TRAVELS BEYOND THE "WEST"

As a child I travelled many times with my family or just my parents to Virginia, Quebec, and northern Ontario, almost always to see relatives. As a young bride, I went with Ron several times to the Maritimes in a Home Hardware sleeper truck. With our four children we travelled to Florida, Winnipeg, the Maritimes and northern Ontario. More recently, as empty-nesters, Ron and I have travelled to many places in Ontario, the US and internationally. But there is one trip that sticks out to me — "Exploring the World of Paul", Turkey and Greece, with Tourmagination, led by Tom Yoder Neufeld and Fred Redekop.

Library at Ephesus

This trip was my first time travelling with a tour group, and also my first experience of travelling in a non-Western culture. From the time we landed in Istanbul we were fully immersed into the Middle Eastern, Muslim culture and way of life. The first evening as my friend Margaret and I walked through the streets close to our hotel, we were a part of the throbbing nightlife that lasts all through the night. Early the next morning we were awakened by the calls to prayer, and the roosters. The imam and the roosters were seemingly in a competition to be the loudest to announce the start of a new day.

The whole trip was a multi-sensory experience. As I look back, I am flooded with memories of the sights, sounds, smells, tastes, and feelings of places and cultures very different from ours.

Frescoe at Meteora

I remember the sights of the ancient ruins: The "old", older still than the old I'd seen before. The viaducts built by the early Romans. Beautiful marble churches and mosques with their exquisite mosaics and frescoes. And blue tiles everywhere; a shade of blue that has ever since stayed on the canvas of my mind.

There were fields of olive trees, breathtaking mountainous vistas, shepherds herding sheep in unfenced pastures, donkeys with their burdens, plodding to town for market day, chickens visiting our table at outdoor restaurants, narrow streets with wash lines strung across some and bougainvillea spanning others, women bent over their hoes in the fields, groups of men talking in tea rooms or playing backgammon with our bus driver while we saw the sights, families gathered around a barbecue in the parks of Istanbul, and marble, marble everywhere.

I remember the animated conversations ending in a friendly slap on the back, the lap of the water against the shore of the Aegean and our voices lifted in praise as we sang the Doxology in the Baptistery of Lydia.

Monasteries high in the cliffs of Meteora

I remember the smell of the salty sea air, the sweet scent of jasmine wafting through the gardens, the incredible mixture of savoury and sweet in the spice market. The tall piles of spices in the marketplace pulled me in with both their fragrance and their beautiful colours.

I remember the flavours that made my taste buds dance — the

freshest tomatoes, watermelon and cucumbers, the baklava, the yogurt so thick that a spoon stood straight up in it, the stuffed peppers and artichokes and falafels and kebabs and grilled souvlaki. Oh, the food! Each meal was a culinary adventure.

I remember the feel of the textiles, the hard, smooth marble, the squish between my toes at the mud spa. I was touched when an elderly woman blessed me for helping her down the steps of the mosque, and I felt awe as I viewed excavation sites that revealed civilizations from thousands of years ago. I felt blessed to have the opportunity to visit and learn.

It was almost mindboggling to see the ancient ruins, to walk down the once bustling main street of Ephesus, to imagine the Apostle Paul walking this same street on his missionary journey. We walked sections of the Roman Way, built circa 300BC (then several years later Ron, Rebecca's family and I walked another short section of it in Northern Italy). The time spent at the Baptistery of Lydia was special to me, seeing the cruciform baptismal area where the convert would shed his old clothes, walk down the steps for baptism, and then don new clothes as he walked up the other side. This visual of stepping down into the waters of baptism, and then rising anew has stuck with me. As we toured the grounds of the Meteora, and learned of the life of the early monks there, I felt challenged by their way of living out their faith. Our tour guide, in describing people of the Muslim faith, often spoke of "the faithful". This was a new expression for me. I had not been accustomed to differentiating the faithful and the secular. Perhaps without using that same word we do the same.

The experience of travelling in this different world and culture was stretching for me, and has given me much to reflect on since that time, perhaps opening a window into the Muslim world to prepare me for later when we welcomed Mujib, Shegofa, the Saeeds, and hopefully soon Shegofa's family. In this time of Covid we no longer take travel for granted. But thankfully, I can look back with gratitude for the travel experiences and the people that I have met who have expanded my window on the world.

26
A TRIP WITH MY MOTHER

I have many memories of good conversations and good times spent with my mother. We had a good relationship. She was my friend as well as my mother. But one memory stands out: when the two of us flew together to Switzerland in June of 1992.

I don't remember exactly how the trip came about, but Mom had voiced a wish to go again to Switzerland to visit Linda, Paul and Ben, and Daddy didn't want to fly again, and with Rebecca completing a stint with Youth with a Mission based in Lausanne, Switzerland, and me wanting to celebrate completing my Bachelor of Arts by taking a trip, it just seemed right.

Plans were made and two seats were booked, flying Swissair June 5th, returning June 19. Our first surprise was when we checked in and found that our economy seats had been switched to business class, with all its perks. Seats at the front with lots of room and close proximity to the washroom, a special little pack with socks and toothbrush and eye covers, and of course a special meal with special service. How did this happen? It didn't take too long to figure out that Margot, Linda's friend who worked for Swissair, had pulled some strings.

I was excited and nervous. This was my first flight to see Linda and the country where she lived, and the first time I was responsible for my mother. The flight was seamless and Mom behaved well.

From the time that Linda picked us up at the airport I was enthralled with Switzerland, and especially the little village of Burg where Linda and Paul and Ben lived. I loved the old buildings, the castles, the cathedrals, the bridges. Architecture that I had before seen only in books and pictures that Linda sent.

Mom, Linda, Rebecca and I stopped in Guggisburg for tea

One of the first evenings we had dinner at Hans and Margot's. They called her "Mam," their Canadian mother. They treated her like royalty, with so much love and warmth, and I was a side beneficiary of their generosity. Rebecca was at that supper too, having arrived shortly before us. In those few months she had been away, she had grown in different ways. I watched her, my oldest beautiful daughter. And it was so good to be together — my mother, my daughter, my sister.

Linda was working at the time, but was so generous in hosting us. She had planned a trip to see the sights and get a feel for the country they called home for many years. We took a few days to travel through the mountains, a bit of the crazy Autobahn, the area around Lausanne that was Rebecca's home for awhile, and way up in the mountains in the Bernese area, to the tiny village of Guggisberg, home of the Horst ancestors. Our first night was spent in Gruyeres, a village with no vehicle traffic. We parked, grabbed our suitcases and walked up the hill to our inn. The raclette we had for dinner that evening was wonderful. Mom shared a room with Linda, and Rebecca and I shared an adjoining room. The views from the Gruyeres castle were breathtaking, looking down over expanses of forest, fields, and the distant mountains.

The next day we headed to Guggisberg. I was excited to see this place that I had researched. I was expecting to walk through the village cemetery and see the gravestones of some of our ancestors, and was surprised to learn that graves are excavated every 25 years to conserve space.

Travelling through the Emmental area we saw other sites of my research — Wahlern, Trachselwald, Langnau. I even snapped a typical Swiss postcard photo of a cow on a hilly pasture, with a backdrop of mountains. Indeed a good trip.

After our return to Burg, we took a day trip into Basel to see the sights and do a bit of shopping. Mom was on the hunt for some lace curtain fabric, and as we walked we saw the opera house where Paul sang, Munster Cathedral, the Rhine River, and the lovely little shops on the narrow streets.

Mom and Linda looking over Burg, towards their home

Another day we crossed the border to France to visit Linda's friend MaryJane at their farm, where they had buildings uniquely positioned to form a square. In the nearby village we visited the pottery shop where I bought a pitcher to add to my collection.

Then, while Mom stayed with Linda to catch up with her daughter, Rebecca and I decided to take the train to the Italian part of Switzerland. To Lugano, Locarno, and Luzern. The Kapellbrucke (1333) and Spreurbrucke (1400s), decorated with 158 oil paintings of Switzerland's history, were amazing. Several years after we visited, the bridges burned down and then were later rebuilt, but we were so fortunate to see the original paintings. As Rebecca and I strolled the palmtree-lined streets and were awed by the sights, we also had time to catch up on the months that we had been apart.

Throughout the whole time Mom seemed to be enjoying herself. There was a sense of relaxation and freedom, and something close to giddiness in her. After all these years I still have a clear memory of Mom, perched up on a barstool at Linda's kitchen counter, gently swinging her legs, merrily chatting, and giggling her unique giggle. The picture of contentment.

While the Swiss scenery was wonderful, beyond anything I'd seen before, the time spent with Mother, Daughter, and Sister was an experience I treasure.

27

RETIREMENT

Retirement felt right when I turned sixty. Ron had retired two years before and in my mind I thought that was lots of time to clean up the sheds and surrounding areas of all the accumulated detritus (read: junk) that he had driven in the lane over the past forty years and we would have the time to spend together to relax after the busy, busy life we had.

When asked what I was looking forward to upon retirement I responded that I would like to have a little hobby farm with many animals for the grandchildren to enjoy. And if there was extra time I would begin studies for my Masters in Theology. Well, fast forward eleven years and that has not happened. I realised that I too had much to sort and disperse, and that is still in the works. Covid helped with this because I was not going away and could dive deeply into the work. The studying initially hit a roadblock when I discovered that I would need a 4-year BA to apply. I was not keen on that and my desire to study has waned as I have realised that life can be even busier in retirement than when employed.

A number of years before my retirement life had become busier as I became part of what is known as the "sandwich generation". My parents were needing more help and I didn't at all begrudge them the time. I wanted to be there for them, and my sisters were there for them too. We helped them to move from their beloved house, had an auction sale of their treasures and "stuff", and then watched in the Spring of 2005 as Mom declined and died, much earlier than we were ready to let her go. Daddy was sinking into dementia already before Mom passed on and confusion hampered any hope of a joyful life for him. In the Fall of 2006 the family met at Linda's for a Thanksgiving meal where Daddy was in good spirits and ate lots of the delicious food, and then a couple of weeks later his life here on earth wound down and he was gone as well.

I learned about a course in Spirituality, "Tending the Soul," that was organized by several churches from MCEC and held at Loyola House. It was stretching for me in some ways, but very soon I realized that it was filling a deep void. The contemplative emphasis helped me in grieving some of the finished parts of my life and encouraged me to move on to what was in the future for me. It was what my soul needed.

And life went on. At the time of my retirement we had three grandchildren, Zoe, Eden, and Simeon. Soon after that Madeline arrived, and then a delightfully busy time when Amelia and Claire were born within four months of each other, and then Quinn followed, and then, finally, along came Ezra. Eight grandchildren! Not as many as my neighbour who kinda lost count at forty-nine, but eight precious souls who pour fresh meaning and joy into our lives. Time spent with them continues to be a gift.

In retirement I got busy with projects that I had started earlier and were waiting to be finished. In some ways I am of the same ilk as my mother and my grandmother. We like to keep our hands busy, but then before we finish one project another interesting one pops up. Some of these half-finished works of art I have sorted out and they have left the house for the thrift shop. Others I would like to get back to. I think I prefer this situation to the one of some of my retired friends who decry the feeling of boredom, especially during the Covid restrictions when we were basically housebound.

Writing is one of my pastimes, especially since taking a writing course at the Senior's Centre. There I was given much encouragement to keep on writing. They were fascinated by the stories I was writing for my family history, and other random writings, and encouraged me to start publishing. After I completed a children's book for the grandchildren one Christmas, one participant scolded me for being selfish and not making more of my work available to the general public. I am still hesitant to put myself "out there" and prefer to write for the pleasure I derive from it. If that is selfish, then so be it.

I have enjoyed writing the stories from the questions that have come weekly to my inbox through Storyworth, which the children gave me as a gift for my big 7-0 birthday. Writing has given my reflections some focus.

Many times we hear that retired life can be very busy. But retirement can provide the opportunity for a simpler life, the choice to slow down.

"*Tis a gift to be simple*" is the beginning of a Shaker folk song, describing a way of life that I find appealing. I think of retirement as the season in life when we can live more simply.

I find simple pleasure in my morning breakfast of porridge, albeit topped with some spiced pear sauce and a liberal sprinkling of walnuts, sunflower seeds, and hemp hearts.

To work with my hands in the soil keeps me simply grounded, and now my "postage stamp" vegetable garden is of a size where I can garden quite simply. My many flower gardens, on the other hand, do not lend themselves to simplicity. But I simply love them.

I find joy in sitting in my sunroom, or on the deck, and watching the chickadees at the feeder, or the butterflies at the butterfly bush, or the hummingbirds drilling deeply into the canna lilies for their nourishment. A simple pleasure.

The first meal of vegetables and fruits of the season — the rhubarb and pears and peaches and tomatoes and corn, is better than a gourmet plate at a high-end restaurant.

I much prefer a walk in the forest in solitude or with a friend, to a crowded, noisy sports event, or even a theatre production.

I prefer my calendar with much free time, as opposed to many spaces blocked off with appointments and engagements, and the busyness of life. During the beginning of this Covid time, when there were stricter rules of distancing, I noticed that my spirit was lighter with the simple life of more solitude and fewer expectations and commitments.

In this second half of life, I find myself opening my hands more often to release possessions, attitudes, roles that had once held importance. To simply pay back, give back to the world a bit of what I have received. And a desire to *"live simply so that others can simply live."* (Elizabeth Seton)

28

CALL THE MIDWIFE

I had the privilege of being a midwife on two occasions, just months apart. The first was helping to bring my granddaughter Eden into this world, and then, just a few months later, helping to birth my father into eternity. Two occasions where my role was to encourage and aid the passage from one life to another; a role that was similar in some respects, yet in other ways very different.

Eden's birth was joyfully anticipated from the time we knew of Rebecca's pregnancy. Our minds were busy with thoughts of girl or boy? What will the name be? and other wonderings. I started the knitting needles clicking and thought of other ways to welcome this new little life.

And then the call came that the baby was on its way. I broke speeding limits to get there on time, and when I arrived Bethany and I had a bit of time to get things in order to prepare for the event. The real midwives seemed to take a step into the background, while all the time watching carefully.

With words and songs and massages we cheered on the passage, growing in intensity with the rhythm of the birthing. And then she was with us, this new little beautiful girl. We whispered, "Welcome, Eden Beth, to our world. It is different from the protection you have rocked in these past months, but we are here to love you through each new experience."

Daddy holding Eden at Thanksgiving 2006

And then, a few months later, I received another call. Daddy was low, and maybe I should come. Again I needed to get there quickly.

Daddy never talked much about dying. Sometimes he despaired of life; other times he refused to be beaten by death. He'd had times before when he seemed low, but then he'd rally. This time seemed different.

This passage was anticipated, but the timing was uncertain and the preparations were different. There were no gifts prepared, although, in hindsight I wish I had knitted a prayer shawl for him. The gifts instead were times spent with him, smiles, re-telling stories, and eating Thanksgiving dinner with the whole family.

Daddy appeared to be resting peacefully when I got to Heritage House where he was staying, but soon he opened his eyes, saw me, and said, "I'm so tired." I responded, "It's okay. Just rest." He gave me a big smile, one I will never forget, and then in a short time he took a couple deep breaths, I stroked his arm and whispered, "Say Hi to Mom, Daddy," and he was gone. Birthed into eternity. From my embrace to God's open arms.

One life arriving.

Another life leaving.

29
THE COVID PANDEMIC

Reviewing the calendar for February 2020, I am reminded that it was a full month — regular yoga sessions, appointments for hair trim, dental, Dr O to remove a spot, meeting with my spiritual companion, meeting with the financial advisor, massage therapy, taking Simeon to *Dogman* show in St. Kitts, comforter knotting, hikers here for lunch of Haystacks, and then at the end of the month was Bethany's surgery for breast cancer. A busy month.

And then things slowed down. When we first heard reports of COVID-19 we didn't pay a lot of attention. It was happening "over there" and we gave little thought to it coming to this part of the world. We were involved mind, body, and heart in helping Bethany and her family through her health crisis.

And then things changed as we heard of the severity of this virus demon, not only just in Europe and Asia, but now in the US and Canada too. This was something to which we needed to pay attention. Then reality struck home as the grandchildren on March Break heard they would not be going back to school right away. Maybe, in a few weeks, the threat of COVID would lessen and they could go back. Weeks became months, and the children stayed home, to learn online lessons monitored by often frustrated parents. Churches were closed, businesses were closed, life out there was shutting down. It was unprecedented.

And then...

And then...

At first we listened to the reports from the government and medical health officials almost daily. We watched the news from around the world and, while we learned this new language, we became more and more confused. We researched previous pandemics — the Spanish flu, SARS — to try to understand. We were not the only ones struggling. The experts themselves didn't always agree. Except, there was agreement that we needed to use hand sanitizer, wash our hands often, and stay six feet apart. Wearing masks was added to the list. And then staying at home, without travelling unnecessarily, was announced.

And how did all of this affect my life? I soon learned that, in this situation, being an introvert was an advantage. I did not feel the loneliness, and the need to go out for coffee, or visit someone daily or weekly. I soon realized the lack of expectations on me. No one would be popping in and notice that I may not have my house-cleaning up to snuff. I could just read a book or do whatever I wanted.

For a while as we watched the daily telecasts and learned of how this disease was spreading, we had *hope* that it would soon be brought under control. But that was not to be. It only became more and more serious.

I joined other sewers in making PPE — first gowns, and then masks. It felt a bit like being enlisted, going to war against this virus. But my life was easy in comparison to people who needed to work at home, often with toddlers running laps around them, and older children who needed help with their online lessons. So many new things to learn. So many adjustments. But also, many people stepping up with creative ideas to make life move more smoothly in this new world.

Hope signs made for the children, using boards from the maple sugar shack

GOING THROUGH SOME THINGS

There are many words and phrases that we have heard time and time again during this pandemic: unprecedented, PPE, social distancing, pivot, Zoom, lockdown, loneliness. But the one I am seeing and hearing more recently is, "I've been going through some things..." At first it would seem that the person is having some medical, financial, or emotional problem, and it could be that in some cases, but what they are really saying is that they are going through THINGS — old cards, old projects, old boxes, old, old, old. And I suppose this is the time that we would be sorting and organizing, trying to chase away boredom, reminiscing, or just finally having time to do some of those things that had been pushed to the back as we've lived our often busy, frantic lives.

I know. I did the same. After sewing the PPE I kept the machine going to do many fun projects — Christmas presents, birthday gifts, humbug bags, durable fabric toys for our dog, Thor that he took as a challenge to methodically tear apart, hoping to beat his last record time to the treat in the middle of the toy.

In this time of COVID, especially now when we are restricted from many activities that we took for granted before the pandemic, spare time has been given to us, if we accept the gift. For some of us who have been keepers (not hoarders, just keepers) we are finding things in wee corners and crevices, things that we had forgotten, which now bring us joy as we walk down the memory lane that beckons us to follow.

Last week my cousin reached out via Facebook to say he had "been going through a few things" and found a letter that I had sent to him, circa 1968, with questions about Quebec separation. Times were tense in Quebec and I wanted to get his point of view as a student in CEGEP in Montreal. Funny that he would still have that letter. Funny that I would still have the essay that I had written on the topic for my grade 13 history course.

Another cousin posted a grade school report card of hers, wondering whether anyone else recognized what it was. Yes I did. And yes, I probably have many of them, perhaps organized by year. Keepers.

Last weekend, while we visited on the deck, Bethany was telling Madeline what a five-year diary was and I was able to walk into the house, directly to the right drawer of the jam cupboard, and get my grandmother's five-year diary. Show and tell. You see, I had "gone through some stuff" a while ago and knew exactly where that diary was. I wish all my things were that easily found.

The list could go on, but suffice it to say that in our efforts to stay home to try to stop this virus, we have the time to "go through a few things." And it is fun to rediscover, and then to reminisce about the time and place of these little bits of history. Some of these "found memories" warm the cockles of my heart. I could do a lot of looking through a lot of things for a long time. But I would prefer to do that without a pandemic.

❧ 30 ❧
PHOTOS ARE GREAT MEMORY JOGGERS

Sorting and organizing photos: the next COVID project and I'm in it up to my ears. Almost 50 years of photos. Some years are semi-organized and some not at all.

We have taken many photos over the years, sometimes in fits and spurts. Not all of our life is represented, but there is enough to give the essence.

Several years ago I had removed photos from older albums before they got "eaten" by glues that were not of archival quality. At that time I had purchased several Michael's shoe box specials and labelled them by year. A good start. But then, over the years, I would root through to find a special photo or three or four, like when I made a scrapbook album for each of the children, and then I was in too much of a hurry to file them back properly. The story of my life. In just too much of a hurry, rushing on to other things. I don't advise it.

Now I am back to those boxes with a different organizational strategy. Most of the photos will stay within their year, providing a good overview of years of our family's activities. But I am pulling the photos of our house and property. I enjoy looking over the years, and seeing the changes, and hopefully improvements, that we have made. Another group of photos that will be pulled are those of any trips that we made as a couple, and as a family, filing them by year, with notations of place, etc.

Our kitchen before and after reno in 1997.

Photos of renovations that we did to our home take time to

look through as they evoke many memories and emotions. The digging out of the basement to provide space for our children to play or watch TV; then tearing down walls on the main floor, providing more open space and making us wonder why we hadn't done it years before; renovating the upstairs to make a larger master bedroom with a walk-in closet, larger closets for the two east rooms, and a cosy little library with a peaked ceiling. And then, years later, when we had saved more money and energy, there was the addition of a sunroom — the room where I spend much of my time — a larger bathroom, with two doors (yikes!), a larger laundry and mudroom, and a double garage. And then the fire, necessitating renovation to the entry room.

The sunroom. My happy place.

Each renovation updated our 1850's farmhouse and opened it up from the small dark rooms. I love our home and will be sad when we will need to say goodbye to it.

Now back to the picture sorting. It is slow going, because I look closely at the photos, and Ron and I reminisce about all the good times. It is quite interesting what a picture can tell about the time, the place, the person. From some photos I am reminded of a very special moment in a person's life. In another picture I see a look on someone's face, and I remember the surrounding circumstances and emotions involved. Photos are a snapshot of real life, after all.

Looking closely at this photo of me as a baby shows that across the road from my family home there were no houses. Just fields and fence posts. I remembered those houses as being much newer than ours but, until seeing this picture, I did not know that I predated them.

I treasure these snapshots of the people and life that are dear to me. I had once said that if we had a fire and I had a chance to grab just a few things, they would be the photos. In fact, when we had a fire there were more pressing things on my mind, and when I wanted to go back into the house the firemen did not allow it. Thankfully the house survived, and the photos did too.

As I call it a day, the table and the floor around the table are covered with photos. I could take a picture of it, to look back on later. But I won't. Because then I'd have to date it, and file it.

31
A MEMORABLE BIRTHDAY

My seventieth birthday is a wonderful memory. A day I will remember for a long time. For me, turning 70 felt like a milestone. I had arrived! And yet hoped for many more years. Celebrations were challenging for anyone in the time of the COVID pandemic. We could not meet together. But that challenge seemed to add fuel to the creative juices of my family, who thought of very unique ways of celebrating. They were very thoughtful in giving what-does-Mom-talk-about-wanting-sometime gifts. The gifts they chose were ones that keep on giving.

I cherish a video that they produced and sent. It is made up of personal birthday wishes from each of the children (I include their spouses when I talk about children — I claim them all) and the grandchildren. I love not only the kind words they say but also the way the video captures the essence of each one of them, in a particular time in their lives. Now, almost one year later, we are still distanced from each other because of the virus, but I can go to my computer and watch the video again, and again, and feel close to my people.

For another gift, they gave me the choice between making mulched paths in the forest at the back of our property, or making a prayer labyrinth. They had heard me talk about wanting each of those. They listen! It didn't take long to decide on the labyrinth. It is close to the house and accessible in all seasons, except when buried by deep drifts of snow. I am so glad that I chose it. I love it.

Everyone was involved in building the labyrinth. First Jonathan and I laid landscape carpet, and then marked the circles. It took me three tries to find a perfect stone for the centre. Ron was very patient in hauling them from the pit. Then each family came, one at a time, and we took a tractor and wagon ride to the back of the pit to collect hand-sized rocks, to line the paths. I can still hear the squeals: "Oh, look at this stone. Look at the colour," and "See the squiggly lines on this one," and "Grandma, look. This is a heart shaped stone. Could I take it home?" We took our load and rode back to the labyrinth site to place the stones carefully on top of the lines for the paths.

Next job was to fill in the paths with some sand, and then we dug in the edging. And then we were done! But, as in many projects, we got ideas for enhancing the look. Over the next weeks Ron and I, with some help, added large landscape stones to make steps down to the labyrinth, and then for a final touch - a barn beam arch. We got the order of work mixed up a bit. The archway and steps should have come first. But that's okay. That is how we do a lot of our projects. I enjoy almost-daily walks on the paths of the labyrinth. It calms my heart and directs my thoughts. It weaves the three-threaded cord in times when it becomes unravelled.

❧ 32 ❧
GOLDEN WEDDING ANNIVERSARY

I still find it hard to believe. Ron and I have been married fifty years!

I was just 10 years old when the family celebrated my Grandma and Grandpa Horst's Golden Anniversary, and I remember thinking they were very old people. Over the years, I have heard the story of how Grandpa said that day, "Fifty years is a long time to be married to the same woman." We giggled when we heard that story, but we knew that Grandpa meant it in the best of ways. Not so many couples in their years had the blessing to be married to their spouse for fifty years. Times were hard for them. They did not have the healthcare that today we almost take for granted. Although many of the family lived to be a ripe old age, it was not always with their first spouse. But now Ron and I are fortunate ones, blessed ones.

Many memories have flooded over me in the past days. Memories of my childhood, of friends and family, of my husband and children, and of the many changes that have taken place over time.

St. Jacobs, the village of my childhood, has experienced great change. The fields across the road and down the hill to Abner Good's flats have changed into growing housing developments. I had taught myself to ski on those hills, using my sister's bear trap skis. The "dump road", where Daddy took me for a drive to tell me about my little Abner chasing a horse and being hit by a car while I was away playing with cousins, is now Printery Road leading past Amsey Bearinger's farm, but cut short from going on to Elo Martin's now by the concrete bridge for the busy expressway.

The flats where I often rode my horse and where Ron and I walked early on the day of our wedding have changed, but happily much of their former self has been retained and enhanced. There is a lovely trail running through. Sometimes through wooded areas. Sometimes along the Conestoga River. It is used by locals and visiting tourists alike. A place where it was a joy to gather with our family, masked and socially distanced, as together we celebrated our anniversary. On a Saturday morning, exactly 50 years from the day of our wedding.

To remain in sadness of the changes and the transformations of my old haunts in St. Jacobs would be a mistake, because this farm where I have lived for 47 years has become even more precious to me than my home in St. Jacobs had ever been.

From the sunroom, my favourite spot in the house, I look out on the beauty of our little part of this big world. In this season I see the corn, growing so tall; the pear tree in its yummy abundance; the colourful flowers in my almost tidy gardens; the birds flitting from tree to tree, singing their reveries, and I write my reflections of gratitude.

RECOLLECTIONS

A WINNER

Whenever I am invited to write my name on a slip of paper and put it in a slotted box to win a prize my response is always the same, "Oh, I never win anything." But that is not entirely true. Actually it is not true at all.

The first win that I can remember was a chicken feeder. A *Purina Feeds* chicken feeder. The details are foggy at best, but I know I was with Daddy and I can picture us sitting in the girls' gym in the basement of the school. I was pretty young, maybe in grade one or two, and I'm not sure why I was there with Daddy. Was it a school event and that's why Daddy was there because he was a school board member and maybe Arthur Schaner (of Schaner's Fuel and Feed who was also a trustee) donated the chicken feeder as a door prize? Or maybe it was a Purina Feeds meeting and that's why they had that kind of prize. I don't know. But I do know that they called out my name and just writing that brings back that queasy feeling in my stomach when I realized I had to walk up to the front to get the prize. Come to think of it, I don't think I even had any chickens. Just a chicken feeder.

It was a little later that I entered a colouring contest for Massey Ferguson tractors. My uncle sold that brand of tractor and one day

Daddy brought home the colouring page for me to try. I did my best with my Crayola crayons. I think I had the big box of colours by then so I was not limited to the standard eight hues, and could really fancy it up with the newer shades and some gold and silver. I was quite pleased with the finished product and hustled off downtown to the shop to give it to them to send away to the contest headquarters. This was big stuff, involving many Massey Ferguson dealerships across Canada, or at least Ontario. I don't remember what the first prize was. I got fifth prize, along with a few other children. It was a large book about horses and dogs. I loved it and kept it until the basement flood of 2018.

Sometimes winning a prize was quite easy, like when the local quilting store offered a door prize to the first ten customers. That kind of win is simple. You just need to get up a little earlier and maybe stand outside in freezing weather for too long and then when they finally open the door you are handed a number which entitles you to a little parcel of things like thread and ribbon and maybe a pattern past its best before date. That prize comes when you check out, having paid way too much for some overpriced fabric.

I also have had some success at stag and doe parties when you have the opportunity to buy a length of tickets which you then tear off and put in a bag in front of whatever prize appeals to you. I once won a set of garden tools that way, and my most recent winning was a bidet attachment to fit on the toilet. You see, the strategy that I have developed is to stuff in tickets only for the things nobody else wants. I really like my bidet.

I have never been one to gamble or buy lottery tickets. The pastor when I was a youth was very opposed to that and it is one lesson that has stuck with me like Velcro. Besides, the feeling I get when I reflect on the "lottery of life" that I have won — my husband, my children, my grandchildren, my home with acreage, my health, my friends — those wins are so far ahead of any amount of money or prizes I could by chance acquire.

Have I ever won anything? Yes. Many times. I am a winner!

MADE TO SHINE, NOT SHRINK

Use what talents you possess; the woods would be very silent if no birds sang there except those that sang the best.
   - Henry Van Dyke

This quote appeared rather serendipitously in the Waterloo Region Record on the very day I received the question from Storyworth, "What are some of your special talents?" I had thought that the answer to this question was going to be quite short, as short as the number of my special talents. But this quote gave me pause.

I was raised in a home where not a lot of praise was given. Too much praise could make one's head swell and could lead to pride, which was among the deadliest of sins for a good Mennonite girl. Later, I learned that to not use our God-given talents ranked close to sin.

From as early as I remember, my mother made most of my clothes. I took for granted that when I was old enough, I would do the same. I remember fashioning doll clothes and simple things and then when I was about twelve I learned how to sew a blouse at 4H club. I enjoyed sewing, especially being able to make something unique that could not be bought at the store, and when I was able to sew clothes for our children it was very cost-saving. I continue to enjoy sewing, especially making quilts, wall hangings, and other special things for the grandchildren.

I began taking oil painting lessons from my mother after I was married. It was something I enjoyed and I felt good about the results. Most of my paintings were landscapes, along with some still life and animals. Now I like to take what talent I have to try some other painting media, and maybe a little more impressionistic style.

Cooking has not always been a joy of mine, and it still isn't the first thing that I do when I have spare time, but I do enjoy trying new recipes, along with the old tried and true. When my husband or children or grandchildren voice their appreciation for a meal, that is the highest praise.

Some people have expressed appreciation for what they call my talent for listening. Above any other this is the talent I desire. It's the one the world and especially those close to me, all need and deserve.

So I return to Van Dyke's words. I take encouragement to use what talent I possess, to give credit to the Source of the talent, and to contribute my best so the woods will not be silent.

I SAW NAOMI DANCING

On Friday morning, December 4, 2020, my aunt Naomi died. She had ninety-five years full of life, and recently she stated, "I just want to go to be with Jesus." And finally she got her wish.

As we so often do after an important person in our lives passes away, I have been thinking of her and her life as I knew it.

Ethel Naomi Snider, born in a farmhouse near Breslau, seventh child in the family of Elias and Sarah (Bechtel) Snider. My mother's youngest sister.

> *This morning,*
> *as I walked the labyrinth,*
> *Naomi was on my mind,*
> *and memories of travelling with my parents to Clayton and*
>   *Naomi's little farm on the Dokis Reserve Road spilled*
>   *out.*
> *Memories of my parents and me sleeping in our station*
>   *wagon,*
> *and getting eaten alive by so many mosquitoes,*
> *the log house being already more than full with Naomi and*
>   *Clayton and their six children.*

*Memories of the few lines in one of Naomi's letters to Mom:
that* "the other day I was getting water at the
pump and I pumped out a snake" *left me totally
flummoxed, and utterly horrified!*
*Memories of my own family, invited to go out in boats on the
French River, and stopping for a shore lunch of the most
delicious spread that Naomi had brought. Salads, at
least four different kinds of them in ice cream pails,
cookies, Freshie, and so much more.*
*And then, as I walked and prayed, I had this image of
Naomi. A younger Naomi, dancing.*

*She danced with freedom,
moving to a rhythm within herself.
It was like she was dancing before the Lord,
and it was beautiful.
I can hear her giggle now,
something like Mom's,
but not quite the same.*

*And I'm not certain what she would say about this image.
But I have an idea.*

*Naomi had a strong faith,
and we often had talks about the things of God,
but I knew that my theology was a bit more left of centre
than hers.
And dancing was probably not at the top of her list of things
to do when she walked through those pearly gates.
But hey, didn't David — not my father or my son, but that
David in the Old Testament — didn't he dance before
the Lord, and the Lord was pleased?*

I'm going to hold on tightly to that image.

NATURE'S SURROUND SOUND

It seemed ridiculous to wake up before five
on a morning free of commitments,
but it didn't take long before I clued into why I awoke so early.
International Dawn Chorus Day, only one day late!

I got my winter coat and a blanket,
and went to the quasi-deck out back and I sat.

At first nothing, save the spring peepers in the swamp,
and the distant drone of traffic
on Wellington 18 and Arthur St North.

And then the first peep — a tentative peep —
and then perhaps it rolls over
for a few more winks of sleep.

A raccoon/groundhog/rabbitty thing
slinks from the field to the red currant bush,
or maybe it is just the floater in my right eye.
It's hard to tell in dawn's early morning.

A call from the spruce tree on my peripheral left,
growing more certain with time.
Perhaps the robin-imam
with the first call to prayer.

An answer comes back from the driving shed roof.
He flies to the wash line post,
and now calls more loudly,
fluffing his wings and stretching his neck high.
I can see his shadow in the growing light.

A rustling in the Mac tree and tentative chirps there —
"Is-it-morn? Is-it-morn?"
Out on the pond the geese are tuning their bagpipes.
"Killdeer, Killdeer," a type-A killdeer wakes up,
already in protective mode.

I hear the sound of the chickadee
and imagine her cute little compact body,
bustling about, doing her Monday chores.

The copse of black locust trees
awake with a chorus,
some reaching tiptoe high notes,
some trilling the medium runs,
and below it all a percussive beat.
Is it the bullfrogs, or a birdsong I don't know?

But my regal cardinal, where is his voice in the chorus?
Not to worry, he will be by later.
He'll fly in about the same time as Norbert and Nora,
the Downys,
coming to begin the day of head-banging foraging.

Monday morning, surrounded by nature's sounds.

CREATION

Sunday morning.
With my cup of tea
I sit on the east deck
and watch the world wake up.

Early sunlight filters through the evergreens.
Dew glistens on the gently waving grasses.

Trees sway in the rhythm of the breeze,
showing off their leaves, all shades of green.
I mix the colours on the palette of my mind —
chrome light green, sap green, a bit of raw sienna.

Corn is growing,
more with each rain,
and each day of warmth.

Birds are busy, cheerily singing their morning praises.
A hummingbird flutters at the feeder,
filled with excited anticipation.

Swallows are foraging their breakfast,
swooping down on unsuspecting insects.
The kingbird and robins preen themselves,
balancing on the branches of the Macintosh tree.

From the line fence my raven gwacks his morning greeting.
A flash of orange and black as the oriole soars by,
then heralds his tune from the pussy willow tree.

And when the great blue heron flies across my sky
I laugh for the sheer joy of it.

Good Morning, God.
Thank you for the gift of creation.

Sunday morning, and all is well.

ADVICE FOR MY GREAT GRANDCHILDREN (AND OTHERS)

Dear Great Grandchildren,

At my ripe age it is thought that I should have accumulated some sage observations and advice to hand down to the future generations. That I don't have much might indicate that I will be around for quite a while longer, to expand my collection. I am trying to think of advice to give to all of you, but it is a bit hard because I haven't met you yet and I'm sure you will all be quite the same, but quite different, so my advice will need to be quite general. (Never use the same word three times in one sentence.)

First of all, though they say this is a strange world we live in, it is really quite a beautiful place. Try to see this beauty, and live with care and respect for the earth. In some places Mother Earth is becoming a bit fragile, so step lightly.

Another thing is that this world is filled with so many people, and people are all different. Be kind, and share your toys.

Find your way into the world of music. And don't give up on music just because your thumbs are too short to reach an octave on a piano. Switch instruments. And be sure to use the handiest instrument you have — your voice. It is hard to feel grumpy when you are singing.

Learn about the people who came before you. Your parents and grandparents and great grandparents. Your life might be different than theirs, but you can learn so much from the lives and times of others.

If you don't read books written by Brené Brown, just remember an important idea she discussed — that people are doing the best they can with what they have at the time. I know, you might not think they are at times, but generally this is the case.

Never go for a walk in a cornfield when you are small. The rows go in circles and you might not end up where you thought you were going. And you can't hear anyone calling because the corn rustling fills your ears.

Similarly, if someday you just feel like leaving home, don't push your wheelbarrow down the ditch on your way to your cousins' place, because your grandpa is sure to see you, and pick you up, and take you back home.

It is good to become familiar with what goes on in the kitchen, and even to make a few things. But don't start your baking by attempting pineapple upside down cake, because it might turn out rubbery, and you might feel like never trying again.

When it says in the Bible that you shouldn't go to bed if you are angry with someone, believe it. You will sleep much better after talking it out.

And speaking about the Bible — get to know it. It is the story of God and of God's people, and you are some of God's people. Read the stories and listen. Talk with others and listen. And talk with God and listen.

My dear great grandchildren to be, I am excited for you. You will see so much, and learn so much, and have opportunities to go many places, and do many things. And remember, Great Grandma is praying for you, especially on rainy Sunday afternoons.

ENOUGH

"Thank you. I have had enough."
When Mujib ate at our table and I asked if he would like more of some dish, his polite reply was, "I have had enough." And it gave me pause each time. This young man from Afghanistan probably had many times in his life when he did not have enough to eat, or enough toys, or clothing, or many of the other things in life that we take for granted. I reflected on times that I was offered more, and my response was, "Oh yes. That was so good. I will have some more."

The desire for more and more can be for food or for other things — lots of clothes, lots of books, a big house, recreational "toys" and much, much love, wherever we can find it. Sometimes we are insatiable.

Several years ago I read *A Life of Being, Having, and Doing Enough* by Wayne Muller, written about the Lord's Prayer. As I think about "enough" I think back to his writings.

In the Lord's Prayer we pray "give us this day our daily bread," but I am realizing more and more that the daily bread is not just food for the day, but rather it encompasses having enough, doing enough, and being enough. We can easily be seduced into thinking that we have not enough, and are not enough. I ask myself if I know what enough feels like, or have I forgotten in the rush of life? I am learning to recognize boundaries — to stop working before I am exhausted, to stop socializing before my inner introvert screams, to stop saying yes; but instead, to calibrate my own inner thermostat. There is a cacophony of noise around us, but by paying attention and listening deeply we can choose to do the next right thing. And each little, tender choice matters.

Perhaps we could say that enough becomes a verb. Through each daily moment we "enough" by listening for what feels right in this one moment. Choices come many times a day, and we make each choice on what is good, what is whole, what is beautiful and holy, and what is, in this day, this moment, enough. And those choices become a thread.

In the poem, *The Way It is* by William Stafford, he begins and ends with the image of the "thread" that weaves through all of life. Through "things that change, but it doesn't change" — so we then ask, what is this "it" which doesn't change. Stafford notes that the thread is something you have to explain to people, because it is hard for others to see. In life bad things happen. Things we cannot prevent. They are just part of "time's unfolding". But, Stafford suggests, you can't get lost because "You don't ever let go of the thread."

And now I come to the end of my stories, my tapestry of threads.

I have enjoyed this year of writing the stories of my life. By diving deeper into some of the questions from Storyworth I was able to recall and reminisce areas of my life that had, for a time, been buried by busyness.

I have not always made choices based on what is good, and whole, and beautiful and holy, so perhaps that has caused some "knots" in my thread. But there are also places where threads have been woven together into a beautiful tapestry, and I thank God for that.

Has my life been enough?
Family, nature, faith.
Planting the seeds.
Watering the sprouts.
Harvesting the joy.
My life has been enough.
Much more than enough.